"A great building—like great literature
or poetry or music—can tell
the story of the human soul."
—Daniel Libeskind

Acclaim for
Breaking Ground

"Less a memoir than a portrait of a life as told through architecture, Libeskind's book traces his past and his numerous project commissions, including his most recent and renowned
contribution to the design of the new World Trade Center.
Tales from his youth in post–World War II Poland and en-
gaging anecdotes about his strong-willed parents, who survived Soviet death camps, are interspersed throughout. For
Libeskind, everything relates to architecture, and the book is
filled with his beliefs about what good architecture should be
and what inspires him. The WTC project has made Libeskind
as much a household name as any architect could wish for, and
with work on the site underway . . . even lay readers may find
this an intriguing introduction to the architect's ideas and in-
fluences."   —*Publishers Weekly*

"Enjoyable."   —*The San Diego Union-Tribune*

continued . . .

"You know right away that Daniel Libeskind's *Breaking Ground*—a collection of insights into architecture, culture, and people, from the guy who designed the master plan to replace the crumbled World Trade Center—is going to be fun when he compares Fort Worth's Kimbell Art Museum with the newbie across the street, the Modern Art Museum. One, he says, is an 'anonymous concrete box.' The other? Nothing less than Beethoven's Fifth Symphony. We won't tell you which is which. You'll have to trek down to the bookstore for that. Here's a hint: It's worth the trip, and the price of the book. . . . The most compelling moments come when Libeskind brings readers behind closed doors, into meetings with others in his firm, with city leaders, and into chance encounters with surviving family members of 9/11 victims. He even is willing to recount tense negotiations and reveal his own occasional doubts. Making readers privy to all this—both the good and bad moments—elevates *Breaking Ground* . . . to invaluable insight into what will arguably become the most nationally significant architectural development Americans will see in our lifetimes." —*Fort Worth Star-Telegram*

"*Breaking Ground* is a surprising and often inspiring book, quite unlike the self-justifying collections of pious clichés that most architects produce when they try to tell their stories. . . . It seems to me an exceptionally truthful book about architects and their lives in the world of expensive buildings and lottery-like competitions. The intimate tone and a certain boyish quality in the narrative create spaces through which interesting truths peek out." —*National Post* (Canada)

daniel libeskind **breaking ground**

An Immigrant's Journey from Poland to Ground Zero

with sarah crichton

riverhead books · new york

THE BERKLEY PUBLISHING GROUP
Published by the Penguin Group
Penguin Group (USA) Inc.
375 Hudson Street, New York, New York 10014, USA
Penguin Group (Canada), 10 Alcorn Avenue, Toronto, Ontario M4V 3B2, Canada (a division of Pearson
Penguin Canada Inc.)
Penguin Books Ltd., 80 Strand, London WC2R 0RL, England
Penguin Group Ireland, 25 St. Stephen's Green, Dublin 2, Ireland (a division of Penguin Books Ltd.)
Penguin Group (Australia), 250 Camberwell Road, Camberwell, Victoria 3124, Australia (a division of
Pearson Australia Group Pty. Ltd.)
Penguin Books India Pvt. Ltd., 11 Community Centre, Panchsheel Park, New Delhi—110 017, India
Penguin Group (NZ), cnr Airborne and Rosedale Roads, Albany, Auckland 1310, New Zealand (a division
of Pearson New Zealand Ltd.)
Penguin Books (South Africa) (Pty.) Ltd., 24 Sturdee Avenue, Rosebank, Johannesburg 2196,
South Africa

Penguin Books Ltd., Registered Offices: 80 Strand, London WC2R 0RL, England

A portion of the proceeds from this book will be donated to Windows of Hope Family Relief Fund, which
was formed to provide aid, future scholarships, and funds to the families of the victims of the World
Trade Center tragedy who worked in the food, beverage, and hospitality professions throughout the
entire complex and who were lost on September 11, 2001. Windows of Hope Family Relief Fund is a
charitable organization; its website is at windowsofhope.org.

The publisher does not have any control over and does not assume any responsibility for author or third-
party websites or their content.

First Riverhead hardcover edition: September 2004
First Riverhead trade paperback edition: October 2005
Riverhead trade paperback ISBN: 1-59448-132-6

The Library of Congress has catalogued the Riverhead hardcover edition as follows:

Libeskind, Daniel, 1946–
Breaking ground : (adventures in life and architecture) / Daniel Libeskind ; with Sarah Crichton.

p. cm.

ISBN: 1-57322-292-5

1. Libeskind, Daniel. 1946—. 2. World Trade Center (New York, N.Y.) 3. Architects—United States—
Biography. 4. Office buildings—Reconstruction—New York (State) —New York—Designs and plans. I. Title

NA737.L46 A2   2004   2004056208
725′.23′092—dc22
[B]

PRINTED IN THE UNITED STATES OF AMERICA

10   9   8   7   6   5   4   3   2   1

To the memory of my parents,
Dora Blaustein Libeskind and
Nachman Libeskind

And to my love, Nina

contents

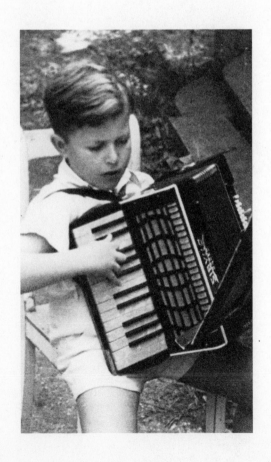

Someone once asked Goethe what color he liked best.

"I like rainbows," he said.

That's what I love about architecture: If it's good, it's about every color in the spectrum of life; if it's bad, the colors fade away entirely. From the ruins of Byzantium to the streets of New York, from the peaked roof of a Chinese pagoda to the spire of the Eiffel Tower, every building tells a story, or better yet, several stories. Think of it: When we consider history, what we see before us are the buildings. Ask us about the French Revolution, and we don't visualize Danton, we conjure the image of Versailles. If we drift back to Rome, what we see first are the Colosseum and the Forum. Standing beside the temples of Greece or near the circle at Stonehenge, we feel the presence of the people who created them; their spirits speak to us across the divide of history.

If architecture fails, if it is pedestrian and lacks imagination and power, it tells only one story, that of its own making: how it was built, detailed, financed. But a great building, like great literature or poetry or music, can tell the story of the human soul. It can make us see the world in a wholly new way, change it forever. It can awaken our desires, propose imaginary trajectories, and say to a child who has seen little and been nowhere, Hey, the world can be very different from what you ever imagined. *You* can be very different from what you ever imagined.

Buildings—contrary to popular thought—are not inanimate objects. They live and breathe, and like humans have an outside and an inside, a body and a soul. So how does one go about designing a building that can sing? A building that expresses character, humanity, and beauty? How does one begin?

One day in the late 1980s, I found myself with one hundred sixty or so international architects in the auditorium of the Berlin Museum, an elegant Baroque building in the working-class neighborhood of Kreuzberg, up against the Berlin Wall. Once, this had been a vibrant part of a vibrant city. Now it was surrounded by housing projects thrown up in the 1960s—a sad, somewhat desolate section of a city divided by a wall, and divided from itself by its tragic past. We had been called here by the West Berlin Senate, which had decided to do something rather brave: to commemorate what had been one of the keys to the city's rich culture—the Jews of Berlin—by adding a Jewish department, within its own extension, to the Berlin Museum.

After a thorough briefing by our hosts, we were led to the site where the wing would be built, a dusty little playground that occasionally hosted traveling circuses. My colleagues snapped cameras furiously, documenting every angle of the angles, but I took no pictures, because I was experiencing something that couldn't be captured on film. As I walked around, all I could think of was everything *but* the site. How can one capture a past so vital and creative, and at the same time so ugly and painful? How can one, using just mortar and glass and steel, capture simultaneously a turbulent past and an unforeseeable future?

A German accent broke through my thoughts. "You are facing East," the man said. "Walk that way, to Kochstrasse, a few minutes, and you will be at Checkpoint Charlie."

The voice was that of Walter Nobel, a nice young man who would soon become well known as an architect in Berlin. "You are new here," he told me gently. "You don't know us Germans. You don't understand how it works. Everything must be done meticulously. You must know the following." He pulled out a pad and began writing down a long series of numbers.

"You must know the toilet measurements. Along with the fire regulations, the toilet measurements are the most important things to know. . . ."

When he finished, I thanked him and tucked his notes into my coat pocket. That evening in my hotel room, as I got ready for bed, I pulled the notes out and tossed them in the garbage. This building would not be about toilets.

Although I have been an architect my entire adult life, I did not actually have a building of mine built until I was fifty-two years old. Now, as I write, six years later, I have three museums completed, including the Jewish Museum in Berlin, and thirty-five projects in various stages of construction. There are museums in Toronto, San Francisco, Dresden, Copenhagen, and Denver; a university building in Hong Kong; a shopping and wellness center in Switzerland; a student center in Tel Aviv and another in North London; and a huge development project in Milan.

I am a lucky man.

How do I know what to design? People often ask me that, and I'm never quite sure how to answer, because my approach is less than orthodox, and even I don't always understand the process. Sometimes my thoughts are triggered by a piece of music or a poem, or simply by the way light falls on a wall. Sometimes an idea comes to me from the light deep in my heart. I don't concentrate solely on what a building will look like, I focus also on what it will feel like, and as I do, my mind becomes occupied by a kaleidoscope of images: the smashing of Joseph Stalin's portrait during the Polish uprising of 1956; the whining of my mother's Singer sewing machine as it chewed up a clump of textiles and spat out undergarments so nude-colored I could barely look; the achingly sweet scent of oranges growing in the Israeli desert; my neighbors, out on their stoops on a hot summer night in the Bronx, red-faced and sweaty, longing for a breeze and arguing over politics . . .

I have led a nomadic life. I was born in 1946 in Lodz, Poland; immigrated with my family to Israel when I was eleven; arrived in New York when I was thirteen. Since then, with my wife and children, I have moved fourteen times in thirty-five years. There are many worlds in my head, and I bring all of them to the projects I work on.

Sometimes, I can be working on a drawing for weeks, making hundreds of sketches, when, with no warning at all, it happens: A perfect form emerges. Several years ago I entered a competition for an extension to the Royal Ontario Museum in Toronto. I had one of those elusive intuitions that are born complete in a moment, and I quickly sketched a few lines and shapes on napkins at the restaurant where I was eating. These napkins ended up displayed on the walls during an exhibition of the finalists, next to fully rendered computer images submitted as "studies" by my competitors. Yet despite my sketches' apparent roughness, compared with the other entries, the building under construction today bears a nearly exact resemblance to them, which indicates that the sketches were as demonstrative of the design and intention of the building as any technical drawing could be. (My wife, Nina—my love, my inspiration, my confidante, my partner, the mother of our three children—says my preferred sketchpads are napkins and paper towels, or anything else lying around. I say she's wrong. It's music paper I like best, because of the geometry of the lines.)

The shape of the extension of the Denver Art Museum, which is being constructed now and will open in 2006, came to me as I flew over the city and could take in its full symphonic presence from above. I am struck by geology—the shifting of tectonic plates, and the unholy forces they unleash, causing whole mountain ranges to be thrust up from the earth's crust. Wrestling with the shape of the museum extension, I copied, in a fashion, the shapes I saw out my airplane window: the craggy cliffs of the Rockies, descending into breathtakingly dramatic valleys and plateaus. I sketched them on the back of my boarding pass, and when that was filled, on the back of the in-flight magazine.

For the Imperial War Museum North in Manchester, England, I struggled to convey the essence of the institution and what it intended to show. It was not about the British Empire, nor was it about war, per se. It was about facing the ongoing nature of global conflict. I had a vision of a globe shattered into fragments, and it was then that I knew what shape the building should take.

I didn't set out to be an architect. I was expected to be a musician, and was in fact something of a child prodigy—an accordion player so good, believe it or not, that I was awarded a prestigious America–Israel Cultural Foundation (AICF) scholarship. I still have a review of a recital held in a Tel Aviv concert hall in which I played alongside a young Itzhak Perlman. The reviewer hardly mentioned the genius violinist, but seemed to have been utterly captivated by the strange, small accordionist onstage, hidden, except for his feet, by his bright red Sorrento, with its silver registers and ivory and ebony keys, the zigzagging folds of its bellows delineated with black and white stripes. The sheer shock of hearing such an instrument play serious classical music made it the center of attention, overshadowing the other instruments onstage.

Even in Poland, the accordion was considered a lowly folk instrument, but we were among the relatively few Jews left in Lodz, and my parents were terrified (with good reason) that if we were spotted bringing a piano into our apartment, we would be targeted by anti-Semites. Since there was little if any serious music published for the accordion, I had to transcribe all the pieces I played. My early repertoire was heavy on Bach, who remains my favorite, but for encores I performed pieces that showed off my virtuosity. My fingers would fly as I played, faster and faster and faster and *faster*, Rimsky-Korsakov's "Flight of the Bumble Bee." In 1953, between hymns to communism, I performed the best pieces from my classical repertoire on the first-ever, black-and-white broadcast on Polish television.

The year I won the AICF scholarship, Itzhak Perlman was also a winner. On the jury sat the violinist Isaac Stern; beside him was the near-mythical Zino Francescatti; and on his other side the divine Mrs. Olga Koussevitzky, wife of the legendary conductor. When I won, Stern took me aside and, in his unmistakable Russian accent, said, "Mr. Libeskind, it is a pity you don't play the piano. You've exhausted all the possibilities of the accordion." But it was too late to switch instruments; my hands were used to playing vertically.

I had always loved to draw, and as the limitations of the accordion grew clearer and clearer, I found myself spending more and more time drawing. I became a fanatical devotee of the pencil. I copied a series of drawings of Hasidic weddings; I drew buildings and landscapes and political cartoons. When we moved to New York, I took a technical drawing course at the Bronx High School of Science, and I loved it. On the days I had class, I would wake up at five a.m., excited by what was in store. After school, I'd finish my homework as I walked home, so that I'd have the rest of the day to practice my technique. I was driven to insane, finger-numbing drawing sessions that lasted well into the night.

My obsessive drawing worried my mother, Dora. She worked in a sweatshop, dyeing fur collars and sewing them onto coats. When she came home at the end of the day, her sweaty skin would be covered with strands of fur, and she would stink of dye chemicals, which we would later blame for the cancer that riddled her body. So disgusted was she by her own stench and appearance that she would refuse to talk to anyone until she'd showered. Then she would emerge a new being, a Jewish mother once again, sleeves pulled back, ready to cook the evening meal in our apartment in the Amalgamated Clothing Workers' Union housing cooperative in the Bronx.

Carp had been a luxury in landlocked Lodz, but was more readily available here, and like many Jewish immigrants, she would buy the fish alive at the market, carry it home in a plastic bag full of water, and let it swim around in the bathtub until it was time to cook it for dinner. I remember how she would drag the bucking carp from the tub and tear out its inner organs, pickle the herring, bake my father's favorite honey cake for dessert, all the while debating literature, history, and philosophy with me. She would offer her wisdom with a sharp wit and quotations from Spinoza and Nietzsche, recited spontaneously in a mixture of Yiddish, Polish, and even English, which was difficult for her but which she delighted in practicing.

One late night she poured us each a glass of tea and sat down across from me at the kitchen table, where I was compulsively drawing. "So you want to be an *ahtist*?" she asked, as if about to make a joke—but she was serious this time. "You want to end up hungry in a garret somewhere, not even enough money to buy a pencil? This is the life you want for yourself?"

"But Ma," I said, "there are successful artists! Look at Andy Warhol."

"*Varhole?* For every Varhole there's a thousand penniless waiters. Be an architect. Architecture is a trade, and an art form." And then she said something that should gladden the heart of every architect: "You can always do art in architecture, but you can't do architecture in art. You get two fish with the same hook."

My brilliant and fearless mother was a profound influence on my life. We are our parents' children, and as someone who was born in the post-Holocaust world to parents who were both Holocaust survivors, I bring that history to bear on my work. Because of who I am, I have thought a lot about matters like trauma and memory. Not the trauma of a singular catastrophe that can be overcome and healed, but a trauma that involves the destruction of a community and its real yet also virtual presence. As an immigrant, whose youth often felt displaced, I've sought to create a different architecture, one that reflects an understanding of history after world catastrophes. I find myself drawn to explore what I call the void—the presence of an overwhelming emptiness created when a community is wiped out, or individual freedom is stamped out; when the continuity of life is so brutally disrupted that the structure of life is forever torqued and transformed.

Mies van der Rohe, Walter Gropius, and the other great modernist masters argued that buildings should present a neutral face to the world, but theirs is a philosophy that feels almost quaint now. Neutral? After the political, cultural, and spiritual devastations of the twentieth century, is it possible to embrace an antiseptic reality? Do we really want to be surrounded by buildings that are soulless and dull? Or do we confront our histories, our complicated and messy realities, our unadulterated emotions, and create an architecture for the twenty-first century?

Buildings have hearts and souls, just as cities do. We can feel the memory and meaning in a building, sense the spiritual and cultural longing it evokes. If you doubt that, think about the heartbreaking immensity of the loss when the Twin Towers of the World Trade Center collapsed.

I was living in Berlin at the time. September 11, 2001—the Jewish Museum had just opened to long lines of visitors. Nina and I felt elated; our job was done. And then came those images, those recurring images. I experienced an indescribable sorrow. I felt a personal connection to those buildings. I had watched them go up. My brother-in-law had worked for many years in one of the towers for the Port Authority of New York and New Jersey, and my father had worked in a print shop nearby. I knew the area well. And because I knew it, during the process of the Ground Zero competition I felt I knew how it should be rebuilt. I envisioned a memorial central to the site, with performing arts, museums, and hotels coexisting with shopping, office towers, and restaurants. I saw streets crowded with life, and the restoration of the magnificent skyline of New York.

But when, later, as a participant in the competition to become the master planner for the restoration of the site, I went to Ground Zero, in one overwhelming moment I realized that the soul of the site existed not only in that skyline and on the busy streets, but down in the bedrock of Manhattan as well.

I had been named a competitor in October 2002, and I was touring the site for the first time. When the bulk of debris had been cleared after 9/11, what remained was a pit unimaginably large, and difficult to comprehend. It was sixteen acres, and as deep as seventy feet. They called it the "bathtub," and Nina and I asked to go down into it. Why, asked our Port Authority guide; none of the other architects had wanted to go. We didn't know how to articulate our response, but we felt it necessary, and so, holding cheap umbrellas against the rain, and wearing borrowed rubber boots, we headed down.

It's hard to explain, yet the lower we descended into the deep hole, the more intensely we could feel the violence and hatred that had brought down the buildings; we felt physically weak with the enormity of the loss. But we could feel other powerful forces present: freedom, hope, faith; the human energy that continues to grip the site. Whatever was built here would have to speak to the tragedy of the terrorist act, not bury it. Down we went, awed by the magnitude of the foundations of the vanished buildings. It was as if we were diving to the ocean floor; we could feel the change in atmospheric pressure. Seven stories of foundation and infrastructure, gone. When the buildings were there, who of us ever thought about what lay underneath? We always think of the skyscrapers of New York, but it's down below where you perceive the depth of the city. Every building stands on such a foundation. Yet who ever touches bedrock? Only construction crews—and then very briefly, before covering it over and moving up.

We were at the bottom of the island of Manhattan, and

we could touch its moisture and coolness, feel its vulnerability and its strength. Where else in a city can you go so low? The catacombs of Rome, maybe. We felt a whole city down there. The ashes of those who died, and the hopes of those who survived. We felt we were in the presence of the sacred.

Then we were up against it: the gigantic concrete wall at the western end of the pit. Later we would see stalagmites of ice bursting from fissures cracking under the pressure of the indomitable Hudson River, seeping through from the other side. "What is this?" I asked our host.

"The slurry wall," he said.

Slurry wall. In all my years of talking with engineers, I'd never heard the phrase. It's a dam—a foundation that is also a dam. Something that should never have been revealed. "If it goes," our host said, "the subways will flood, then the whole city will be underwater."

"An apocalypse."

"Yes."

It loomed over us, appearing bigger than any building we'd ever seen, and as we stood in that vast pit it felt almost infinite, the embodiment of everything—what collapses, what is resilient; the power of architecture; the power of the human spirit. It was many colors at once, patchwork overlapping patchwork, because over the years the wall has often had to be reinforced so that it wouldn't collapse. It was haptic, tactile, pulsing, a multilayered text written in every conceivable language.

Looking up, I could see people standing along the edges

of what seemed like cliffs above, craning their necks to peer down into the site. That's when I understood that what I had to do was design a scheme that would draw up out of the New York City bedrock. A ray of sunlight cut through the clouds. How did it reach so far down? I needed to make sure that sunlight was a part of the design too. I thought of the little American-flag pin my father wore in his lapel long, long before 9/11. I thought about my first sighting of the city skyline, as the boat I was on steamed into New York Harbor in 1959. I could see myself as a thirteen-year-old, in a crush of immigrants, staring up slack-jawed at the Statue of Liberty.

"Call the Studio," I told Nina while we were still in the pit. It was late back in Berlin, where we had our headquarters, but our staff there was still hard at work. "Drop everything that you've been doing," I told them. "I have a new plan."

How do I know what to design? I listen to the stones. I sense the faces around me. I try to build bridges to the future by staring clear-eyed into the past. Does this sound overwrought? I hope not, because buildings should never be maudlin or nostalgic; they should speak to our time. I am inspired by light, sound, invisible spirits, a distinct sense of place, a respect for history. We are all shaped by a constellation of realities and invisible forces, and if a building is to have a spiritual resonance, it has to reflect these things. No one knows how body and soul are connected, but connect them is what I try to do. I draw from my own experience— it's what I know—and in doing so, I strive for a universality.

·2

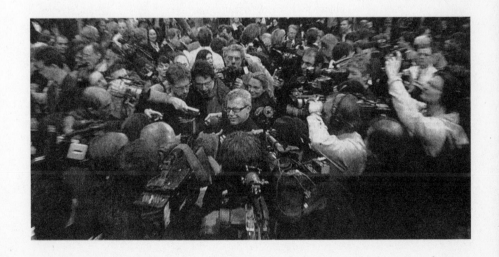

a sense of
place

All architects are prostitutes—that's what Philip Johnson said; they'll do whatever it takes for the chance to build. Frank Lloyd Wright put it a little less brutally. He said there are three things an architect should know: Number one, how to get a commission. Number two, how to get a commission. Number three, how to get a commission.

It's a cynical take on a profession, certainly, and as the son of two idealists and the husband of another, I'd like to argue that not *every* architect lacks principles. But I've also had to face the fact that there's a lot of truth to what the masters said. Unlike artists or philosophers or writers, architects are totally dependent on others—others with money, and lots of it, because it's expensive to put up a building, even a modest one. That, to cite Philip Johnson again, is why it's so tempting for architects to become the pawns of the powerful. And any doubt I had about this was blown away in September 2002, during the Venice Biennale of Architecture.

Here in Venice—in the phantasmagoric city that celebrates the fact that anything, absolutely anything, is possible in architecture—much of the architectural world had gathered for an international exhibition built around the theme "Next" (poignantly appropriate, given what had happened a year earlier). People love the Venice Biennale. If invited to participate, only fools turn it down; it's much too beautiful and too much fun to pass up. Nina and I were there with Carla Swickerath, a senior architect in our studio. We had several schemes on exhibit. By day, we toured fellow architects' exhibits in the pavilions; by night, we drifted from opening to opening, loading up on canapés and Prosecco and working the rooms.

Deyan Sudjic, architecture critic for the London *Observer* and the Biennale's director, took me aside in the Palazzo Venier dei Leoni, the Guggenheim museum on the Grand Canal. "Daniel," he said. "Tomorrow morning. Panel discussion. On the World Trade Center site—"

How appropriate. I had that very day gotten a call from Alexander Garvin, vice-president for planning, design, and development for the Lower Manhattan Development Corporation, inviting me to sit on the jury to choose, first, the architects who would compete to redesign Ground Zero and, later, a winning scheme. I was deeply honored and excited by Garvin's proposition—and intrigued by Sudjic's invitation.

"Herbert Muschamp will be there," Sudjic continued. "Jean Nouvel and Zaha Hadid are coming too. Many others. Join us. Sit in the audience. Very relaxed. Maybe comment on what you hear onstage."

I like Jean Nouvel very much; he's an elegant and clever man, a European version of a high-tech architect, best known for the Institut du Monde Arabe, built on the banks of the Seine in Paris, with its light-sensitive façade that resembles the irises of many eyes. I admire Zaha Hadid too. The last time I saw her she had a shiny gold purse shaped like buttocks, molded out of some very expensive material and looking absolutely lifelike. Zaha has her own bold style. Being an architect has not always been easy for her, as an Iraqi woman in a world that's still almost exclusively male. But she's inventive, and she's stuck to her ideals and by her ideas—and it's working, she's succeeding. It's shocking that architecture is still so male. But as with all fields, that will change, and architecture will change as a result, because the women will draw on their own experiences, and bring with them new perspectives. What does that mean? Well, we'll have to wait and see, won't we? I look forward to it.

Jean and Zaha; yes, they'd make very good company. Herbert Muschamp, on the other hand, is more of a mixed blessing. Muschamp was, until recently, the architecture critic for *The New York Times*, which, because of its national and international stature, made him almost terrifyingly influential, and he wrapped his power around himself like a luxurious fur-lined cloak. Architects will do anything to win his heart.

Unless they are among those who are frequently featured in his articles—Peter Eisenman, Rem Koolhaas, or Zaha Hadid, say. His internal compass seems to swing quixotically. One minute he loves you; the next he's not seeing you; and the next you're toast. Nina and I had breakfast with him at his fancy hotel one morning in Venice, and we were amazed—and amused—to see the architects aiming for a spot near our table. You could feel them swarming, buzzing, drawn inexorably to him, like bees in a hive. He gave me a book not too long ago, on Eleusis and its dark mysteries. I don't know why he thought it would speak to me. He inscribed it, "From Herbert with love."

His power feels excessive to me.

The last time I had seen Muschamp before Venice was in Berlin in the late 1990s, when he came to check on the progress we were making with the Jewish Museum, and to write about Norman Foster's reinvention of the Reichstag for the German Parliament, with its gleaming metal-and-glass dome. It had been arranged that Nina and I would pick him up at his hotel and take him to dinner, but when we called his room, he answered, "I'm terribly sorry, I'm still in the tub." And he stayed in the tub. It was an hour before he climbed out, and when he finally did join us, he was so *extremely* relaxed it proved somewhat difficult to conduct a conversation with him.

Yes, a panel on the future of the World Trade Center site—this would be most interesting. Of course I would go.

Venice glistens in times of celebration. Leaving Nina and Carla to the parties, I slipped into a narrow alley behind the palazzos, headed over a handful of bridges and across a few less-traveled piazzas, until I came to the place: a pier, now seemingly unused, at the end of the Grand Canal. It was here that my parents, my sister, and I had boarded a Greek container ship that looked like something out of a World War II movie, to go to Israel in 1957. This was the jumping-off point for our new lives after making it through the Iron Curtain. At the time, we didn't have the luxury to stop and look around— Venice was nothing but a transit point on the way to freedom. Now I could pause to delight in its extravagant beauty and the imagination behind it.

As I doubled back to the parties, I thought about how it's said that time flows like water—and it does. But that doesn't mean it flows *evenly*—it zigs and zags, slams against rocks, gets dammed up and bursts down waterfalls. . . .

I thought back to 1989. Nina and I had moved with the kids to Berlin that summer to try to get the Jewish Museum built. Eastern Europe was exploding, triumphing at last over the legacy of Joseph Stalin. The previous April, the Hungarian government had cut its wire fence along the border with Austria, a fact not lost on the East Germans, who voted aggressively with their feet as they went on vacation in Hungary that July and August. They ran on into Austria, where the Red Cross would pick them up and repatriate them to West Germany. Hundreds more, who couldn't get over the border, were occupying the West German embassies in Prague and Budapest. The most desperate of all, East Germans who couldn't get to Prague or Budapest, had taken up occupation in the West German diplomatic mission in East Berlin.

I was at a dinner that fall with a prominent German historian. "What do you think will happen here?" I asked the great professor.

"Pfffftt," he said, with a dismissive shrug. "It doesn't matter what instability is over there. The Wall will stand for another hundred years."

A month later, on November 9, 1989, our two sons, Lev, then twelve, and Noam, ten, were rushing into our apartment to grab hammers, and racing back outside with me and their baby sister, Rachel. I remember hoisting her on my shoulders so that she wouldn't be crushed in the crowd of tens of thousands of Germans, who, with the Pink Floyd song "The Wall" blasting from nearby, converged to help bring the hateful Wall down.

Nobody had foreseen this happening. Not two weeks before, not one day before.

November 9, 1989. In one day, a terrible era ended.

Twelve years later, our family was still in Berlin, and we had cause for two celebrations: our daughter's bat mitzvah and, at very long last, the official opening of the Jewish Museum Berlin. On September 8, Rachel was called to the Torah under the golden Moorish domes of the grand Oranienburger

Strasse synagogue, and that night, the museum was fêted with
a concert and a dinner attended by all of Germany's leaders,
including President Johannes Rau and Chancellor Gerhard
Schroeder. The next day, the dignitaries toured the museum.
And on Monday, September 10, on a boat cruising the canals
of Berlin, we threw a joyous bash for more than a hundred
people who had worked so hard to get the museum built.

The next day, after twelve years of fitful legal wrangling
and painstaking construction, the fully installed Jewish Museum Berlin opened its doors to the public. For a few hours.
And then, like so much else around the world, it shut down.
It was September 11, 2001. And as with the Berlin Wall, no
one had foreseen it happening. In one day, a terrible new era
had begun.

What do you do if you've just witnessed one of the most dev-
astating horrors in modern memory? Only six weeks before
terrorists slammed airplanes into the Twin Towers, Larry
Silverstein had completed a transaction to lease the commercial space in the buildings of the World Trade Center
from the Port Authority of New York and New Jersey. He
wasn't a well-known developer; most New Yorkers had never
heard of him. But in one day, Silverstein became, in the
words of the city, a big deal.

David Childs, partner and lead designer at the gargan-
tuan corporate architecture firm Skidmore, Owings & Mer-

rill, was one of the first people Silverstein talked to. Childs told Silverstein he was ready to rebuild the towers—a statement that made many people furious when they heard about it. It felt crass to them that these men were talking real estate when thousands lay dead, when it was still hoped that more survivors might be pulled from the burning rubble.

"Oh, yes," Childs told *The New York Times*—with, as the reporter described it, "unassailable cheer"—"I was a pariah for a time." He got so many hate calls he had to change his cell phone number, but eventually, he said, "people came around."

This is what happened next: In July 2002, the Lower Manhattan Development Corporation (LMDC), a state agency created after 9/11, and the Port Authority unveiled six plans for rebuilding the towers. It was a debacle. The proposals were devised by a local architecture firm, Beyer Blinder Belle (although one originated as a Skidmore, Owings & Merrill design). All were awful. Herbert Muschamp wrote in the *Times* that what was displayed was "a breathtaking determination to think small. Don't come looking for ideas that reflect the historic magnitude of last year's catastrophe. Nor will you find any sign of recognition that ground zero has become a tragic symbol of the troubled relationship between the United States and the rest of the world. What you see, instead, are proposals for real estate development: six ways to slice the pie."

About this, there was universal agreement. A few days later, a town hall meeting was held to let the public air its views. And did it ever. Some five thousand disgusted and vocal New Yorkers showed up. When asked to vote on the six designs, the audience rated each one "poor."

The LMDC announced that it would rethink the rebuilding process. At the same time, Muschamp jumped into the game by announcing that the *Times* would sponsor an architectural study to "reimagine" the future of lower Manhattan, and that he had assembled a consortium of architects, urban planners, and designers to come up with new visions that would be presented in a special issue of the *Times Magazine* in September.

Muschamp was here in Venice to preview the contents of the magazine, which would be published in a matter of days. The panel was to address the designs that would appear in the magazine.

When you come to the Venice Biennale, you tend to stay up late and sleep in. And if you are a cutting-edge architect you stay up even later, and are not seen before noon. The panel was scheduled for mid-morning; it was therefore sparsely attended. Zaha and Jean were no-shows, and those who did make it seemed a bit dazed from the river of Prosecco the night before. But Muschamp was there, as were his friends the architects Frederic Schwartz and Steven Holl; both had participated in his *New York Times* project. Billie Tsien, who, with her husband, Tod Williams, heads the New York firm

Tod Williams Billie Tsien and Associates, was representing the LMDC. And there was Roger Duffy, senior architect at Skidmore, Owings & Merrill.

Once SOM was the sort of architecture firm that big American corporations turned to whenever, for example, headquarters needed designing. But in the last decade the firm had lost its luster. People found its designs unimaginative and sometimes dull.

Attempting to repair the firm's sagging reputation, Duffy took an unusual gamble. He assembled a panel of outside evaluators, including the artist Jenny Holzer, the architect Jesse Reiser, and the architectural historian Kenneth Frampton, and asked them to critique some of SOM's top projects. He then published their evaluations, uncensored, in book form and made them available to the public. It was a risky move, and it didn't entirely pay off, because some of the critiques were especially blunt. But it did get people talking about SOM again.

Now Larry Silverstein had awarded the firm the commission for 7 World Trade Center, to replace Tower Seven, which, though not on the World Trade Center superblock, had collapsed more than eight hours after the 9/11 attack, victim of collateral damage from the Twin Towers. But SOM had even more at stake here. One way or another, it wanted to be responsible for rebuilding all of Ground Zero.

The lights dimmed, the slide projector hummed, and with Deyan Sudjic moderating, the panelists began to talk. They weren't particularly lively, but the slides were interesting.

SOM offered a plan that featured a bunch of dense, loopy towers. It was certainly more imaginative than the hulking glass box slated for 7 World Trade Center, and it was an attempt at meaningful design—but it failed. To me it was just more meaningless form-making.

The Muschamp group fared better. After his handpicked consortium of architects had more or less agreed on an overall plan for lower Manhattan, Muschamp had assigned each of them a specific project. He'd asked Richard Meier to design a school; Steven Holl, a museum and a theater; Rafael Viñoly, a transit hub; Zaha Hadid, housing. The Mexican firm TEN Arquitectos suggested combining housing and a library in two attached towers, with staggered terraces in various colors.

Well, at least this is better architecturally, I thought. And then I was overwhelmed with a different, sickening thought: Something was wrong with what we were looking at. Really, very wrong.

So much was being said about what had happened at Ground Zero, but so little was being conveyed by the architecture itself. Almost three thousand people had died, and we were treating the site of the tragedy as a tabula rasa, a clean slate to be filled with fashionable buildings. Asked to design an office building, Rem Koolhaas took a satirical look at New York's supposed obsession with Art Deco, and turned three buildings upside down, which not only made them seem trendy, but also meant extra space for the more desirable and expensive higher floors.

The designs were so *current,* so *smart,* and everyone was feeling so very, very clever. . . .

Sudjic's voice cut through my thoughts. "Mr. Libeskind, would you like to come to the podium and say a few words?"

Say what? Start where? End how? I came forward slowly. First I thanked Sudjic and the panel for their interesting discussion. I congratulated Herbert Muschamp on his ability to bring all the architects together in such a congenial fashion. And then the words stopped coming. Not because I didn't know what to say, but because I was speechless, clearly on a different wavelength from the others in the room. "I need a moment to think," I said, burying my head in my hands as I struggled for composure. Two minutes passed. The audience sat silently, studying me. Was this theater? No. It may have seemed theatrical, but it wasn't for show.

"I can't help feeling a little like I'm watching the Emperor Nero fiddle as Rome is burning," I said. "It's very nice to have beautiful renderings and beautiful buildings back on the site and not to have architects building banal, pseudo-functionalistic things there—and it's nice to have good housing and clever office buildings, with nice forms and so on, but what I would ask for is something more profound."

"What should be the goal here?" That's what I asked the audience, which had now grown alert, and the panel, which had grown tense. "Is it to erase the memory of what has happened? Is it to show that everything is fine? That everything will be just as it was before?" Glossy, contemporary, ironic, self-satisfied architecture isn't the answer, I said. "One needs a more profound indication of memory."

What we needed, I concluded, was "a dramatic, unexpected, spiritual insight into vulnerability, tragedy, and our loss. And we need something that is hopeful."

I had said enough. I felt I had to get away from there. I bolted from the stage and headed straight out the door. Nina, moved by my outburst, and ever the peacemaker, ran up to Muschamp to try to make amends. "I'm sure we can get things straight," she told him, and agreed we'd meet him for breakfast the next day.

By the time evening came around and the parties started, I'd calmed down. But not everyone had. I was catching up with Vivian Bennett, an old friend from our time building the Imperial War Museum North in England. Carla Swickerath appeared with goblets of red wine for everyone, and out of the corner of my eye, I saw Nina laughing nearby with Billie Tsien and Tod Williams. Then suddenly I saw Fred Schwartz, Viñoly's sidekick, push through the crowd. His eyes were bloodshot; his face was contorted with anger. The unshaven face of an angry man is a frightening sight. He bore down on me, grabbed my collar, and started to shake me. "I'm a New Yorker, *damn it!*" he growled. "Don't tell *me* how to build my city!"

"I'm a New Yorker too . . ." I said quietly, trying to wrench free. He looked like he wanted to punch me; I braced myself for the blow.

"You think you can stomp all over us?" he yelled.

"I wasn't the one doing the stomping, Fred. I was simply asked to comment. And that's what I did. I disagreed with you."

Carla threw her weight between Fred and me to make him stop, while Nina tried a gentler approach. "Fred, take it easy. Let's just talk about this."

"I don't have anything more to say to either of you," he spat, before finally letting go and disappearing back into the crowd.

"I think a long gondola ride would be nice right now, don't you?" said my wife. With one hand she took my arm, and with the other she grabbed a bottle of champagne and steered me out into the night. My wife is a genius.

Americans hear my accent—which is Polish and a bit Yiddish, I think—and make assumptions. *He's foreign,* which, yes, at one point I was. Like so many other New Yorkers, I wasn't born in the city. But my parents' search for a home—which took them from Poland to the Soviet Union, back to Poland, and then to Israel—came to a happy end in New York by the close of the fifties. In our strange loop through Israel, the Libeskinds were repeating the ebb and flow of the Jewish people. We were Israelites, arriving in the Promised

Land, but we were also Joseph, leaving it. Our real promised land would be New York City.

My first vision of the city was so iconic that at times it feels as if I assumed it from an old RKO newsreel. I didn't, though. I lived it. We were among one of the last waves of immigrants to arrive in the United States by boat. In the summer of 1959, we sailed into New York Harbor on the *Constitution*, my mother and my older sister, Ania, and I. My father had made his journey a few months before. It was early morning when my mother shook us awake and led us up through the crush of people on deck, so that we too could stare in awe as the Statue of Liberty and the magnificent New York skyline emerged out of the dawn mists. For some Americans, the Statue of Liberty has become a cliché—a pawn in a political tug-of-war, too eagerly embraced by the right, rejected as sentimental patriotic propaganda by the left. But if you are an immigrant kid, it is the most incredible sight: Lady Liberty pointing her torch to the sky. You behold the promise that awaits you. As for the skyline, the tremendous success story of America is almost palpable in its grandeur.

My father, Nachman Libeskind, had already fallen in love with New York in the months before we arrived, and when we disembarked, he was eager to introduce us to our new home. As we walked, every person in the street looked to us like a hero, a god. These were Americans! These were the people who had beamed us Radio Free Europe, which broadcast illegally out of our clunky old Polish radios. My American-born friends tend to dismiss Radio Free Europe as propagandistic tripe; they will never understand that in fact it was a godsend. The news it aired was the only truth we got about the world. On our third day in New York, my father took us to Radio City Music Hall to catch Hitchcock's *North by Northwest* on what was then the biggest screen in the world. The Rockettes! Cary Grant dangling from the noble nose of George Washington, carved into Mount Rushmore! There they were, the pantheon of great Americans: Washington, Jefferson, Theodore Roosevelt, Lincoln. Who cared that we couldn't understand English? *This* was the American Dream, and I was living it.

Here at last was a city in which everyone in the world could be equally at home. I can remember how surprised I was to hear Yiddish freely spoken in the streets. In Lodz, where the remaining Jews were barely tolerated after the war, it was a language that one kept hidden. I would often walk with my father around Lodz, aware that he inhabited two cities at once, that of the living and that of the dead. He walked among invisible shadows, looking for other survivors, others who inhabited his ruined world. When he passed someone who looked familiar or who he thought might be a Jew, he would whisper *"ahmhoo"*—the Ashkenazi pronunciation of the Hebrew for "one of the people." It had become a kind of password among Polish Jews, and if it was recognized, the two would break into quiet Yiddish; they would ask about the fate of acquaintances or reminisce about the time before the war.

You might think it would have been different in Israel, but

Yiddish was verboten there as well. The language was part of a world everyone had left behind, and if we slipped into it on the streets of Tel Aviv, someone would invariably shush us. "Don't talk that loser language. You're not in Poland anymore. This is Israel. Enough of that."

In New York, though, anyone could speak any language—and did.

After a brief, miserable stint in a belt-making factory, my father found a job in a print shop owned by a rabbi, blocks from the future site of the World Trade Center. Here, on Stone Street, he worked happily for more than twenty years as a photo-offset stripper. The process he used is almost extinct now, and involves extraordinary patience, and coordination of hand and eye. Always a stickler for order and precision, he got so good at aligning pictures and texts that he dispensed with a ruler completely: his eye and hand ruled the galleys; he had mastered the line in his mind.

There was water on the floor, there were rats in the building, the wages were low, and every day he had to haul paper from the warehouse to the print shop, but Nachman never complained. He loved America. When my mother was dying, she made him promise that he would start to paint. "You've always wanted to," she said. "Now is your time." And so he did, producing hundreds of paintings, and enough fine ones to mount his first one-man show when he was in his mid-seventies. He never painted landscapes or anything sentimental. His work wasn't the work of an old man. His paintings were hard-edged, abstract, shocking really, sharp and bold. It wasn't until I stood in the middle of the gallery at my father's first opening that I realized how often he incorporated the colors of the American flag and images of the Statue of Liberty into his art.

On returning to Berlin from the Venice Biennale, I realized I had a prior commitment that would make it impossible for me to accept Alexander Garvin's invitation to serve as a juror for the World Trade Center competition. I was scheduled to be in Toronto the week the jury would meet—I had an unbreakable date at the Royal Ontario Museum. I was disconsolate. Carla was thrilled. "Oh, Daniel," she said. "This is actually good news. It means we can enter the competition, instead."

The young man I'd spoken to at the LMDC when I called to turn down the jury position had said much the same thing, but I'd brushed him off, and now I brushed Carla off with a list of reasons why it was too much of a long shot: We had less than three weeks to pull an entry together; the New York architecture scene seemed to have the commission locked up; we hadn't been invited to compete; and, and, and . . .

We submitted our entry with moments to spare. A few weeks later, Nina and I were sitting in a quiet corner of the Toronto airport, waiting for our delayed flight to New York, when Nina's cell phone rang. It was Carla calling from Berlin. "I should have bet you the store on this one!" she said.

We had been short-listed as one of seven competitors for the design study. My heart danced. And the madness began in earnest. It was time to go home—not to Berlin, but to my real home, New York.

The Jewish philosopher and theologian Martin Buber used to tell a story, a variation of which I've found in Hindu literature. In Buber's telling, a poor Jew dreams one night that if he leaves his shtetl and goes to Prague, he will find gold treasure buried for him at the foot of the Charles Bridge. So, being both a poor Jew and a true believer, he grabs his spade and walks and walks and walks until he finally comes to the bridge. Sentries guard it, but he has no choice: he gets to work digging.

A large sentry soon looms over the poor Jew. "What do you think you're doing?" he growls.

The poor Jew replies, "Right there, right on that spot where you're standing, I dreamed that there is gold treasure buried."

The sentry laughs. "That's funny," he says. "Last night, I had a dream that in a poor shtetl there lives a Jew, and in his hut, under the hearth, is buried gold treasure." So the Jew returns home, and starts excavating, and sure enough, he finds the gold.

The moral, as I take it, is that sometimes you have to leave home for a while in order to recognize the treasure that is there.

———

The seven finalists were called to New York in mid-October for a briefing by the LMDC and the Port Authority.

At the time, New Yorkers were deeply divided over whether or not to rebuild at Ground Zero. To many, this was hallowed ground, and they didn't want to see its history erased or paved over. It was easy to understand their reluctance. But the site could not be left as it was. Ground Zero is in the heart of Manhattan's financial district; it was psychologically as well as economically vital to provide the area with a future, to move on from its traumatic past. John Whitehead, the LMDC chairman, was asking for master plans that would address both the philosophical and the emotional questions raised at the site (his brief was entitled "What Does September 11 Represent?") while tackling critical practical problems raised by the destruction of the towers. There were pressing transportation concerns. The original design had cut the World Trade Center off from adjacent neighborhoods, and at night, the superblock was barren and lifeless. How could this now sacred place be integrated into the city? How could life be brought to these streets? There was another, cruder issue: Larry Silverstein insisted that above all else he was entitled to 10 million square feet of rentable retail and office space to replace what he'd lost.

Master plan proposals would be submitted and judged in eight weeks. Then, it was hoped, the process of restoration and healing could begin.

One of the seven finalists was Foster and Partners. Lord Norman Foster, who arrived in New York for the LMDC's briefing with a large entourage, is a suave Englishman, a technical genius, who travels with dozens of little sketchbooks into which he constantly jots ideas. He figured out how to fuel Berlin's Reichstag dome with vegetable oil, thereby reducing carbon dioxide emissions by ninety-four percent. He stretched a delicate steel-and-aluminum frame for London's first dedicated footbridge across the River Thames. At first the Millennium Bridge had so many pedestrians that it wobbled, and some walkers felt seasick, but engineers were called in to repair it. Foster's Hongkong and Shanghai Banking Corporation tower in Hong Kong (he's built a lot there and in Singapore) is one of the most high-tech buildings in the world. It is also said to have been the most costly. Foster is undoubtedly one of the busiest architects in the world, and a great businessman. He was raised in the working-class Levenshulme district of Manchester, and in a tale that is far more U.S. than UK, he succeeded in crashing through class barriers.

Years ago, Nina and I were invited to a party at his immense apartment in London, which has its own helicopter landing pad and a two-story-high library. His dining table is a good twenty feet long. I was standing at a window, looking out on the lovely, curving Thames, when Lord Foster came over. "There's something I cannot forgive you for."

I couldn't imagine what it might be.

"The Imperial War Museum in Manchester," he said.

"But it's such a tiny project!" I protested. "They only gave me twenty-five million dollars to build it with."

"But that's my town," said Lord Foster.

He and Fred Schwartz. Ah, the proprietorial connections we have regarding place.

Schwartz was also a competitor, as one of a group that called itself THINK and consisted of Rafael Viñoly, Shigeru Ban, Ken Smith, and David Rockwell. I had settled into a seat in the briefing room when Viñoly walked in. We had never met, and I didn't see him enter, but as he did, he slapped me on the back unusually hard, saying, "So, Mr. Architect is too famous to say hello?" It gave a hint of some contentious times to follow.

SOM (with the help of another group, SANAA) was another of the seven, as was a small local husband-and-wife firm, Peterson Littenberg. United Architects, another of the competitors, was an international team of young, experimentally minded architects, including Jesse Reiser (who had been my student at the Cranbrook Academy of Art), Ben van Berkel (I was on a jury that awarded him an important commission), Kevin Kennon, and Greg Lynn. Another team included some former teachers of mine: Peter Eisenman, Richard Meier, Charles Gwathmey, and Steven Holl had pooled their talents, and were calling themselves "The Dream Team," which took audacity, but they are an audacious group.

I had studied at Cooper Union with both Meier and Eisenman, and I had sort of worked for each of them too. In the late 1960s, Meier was part of a loose-knit group of avant-garde architects and theoreticians who came to be known as "The New York Five." The other four were Charles Gwathmey; Michael Graves; my mentor and friend John Hejduk, who was dean of the school of architecture at Cooper Union; and Peter Eisenman, who headed the group. My first job, in 1968, was as an apprentice to Meier, who is now perhaps best known for the Getty Center in Los Angeles, and who at the time was already creating the striking white geometric neo-Corbusian designs for which he has become famous.

Like his buildings, Meier's office was sleek, machinelike, hushed. The apprentices sat at their desks with copies of the master's book *Richard Meier: Architect* propped before them, silently copying, over and over, the curves he'd made in his forms. After a day of this mindless, robotic action, I thought, This is not for me. But what to do? The next day I called in sick. And the day after that. And the day after that. After a week of absence, Meier called me at home. "Are you really sick?" he asked.

"Richard," I said, "I have to tell you the truth. I just can't do this. It's not what I believe architecture should be, it's not what I want to do."

Eisenman has been described in many ways—brilliant, iconoclastic, inventive—but no one has ever called him a mensch. Even though I had been his student, I wasn't entirely prepared for my first day working for him at New York's Institute for Architecture and Urban Studies, which he founded. I had just finished my postgraduate degree in England and arrived back in New York with Nina, flat broke.

Not only did Eisenman offer me a job, he promised to give me a check on my first day to tide us over. But when I showed up, he handed me a broom and told me to sweep the office. It was a demeaning initiation, a forced act of submission. I was there to do architecture, not sweep, so I refused.

"You want the check—or not?" he asked, holding it up in front of himself.

"Keep it," I said, and walked out. We didn't talk for another decade.

I was young, and I may not yet have had a clear sense of my place in the world. But I did know that mindless copying and sweeping floors were not it.

A sense of place. It is an inviolable thing, whether you're talking about where a person belongs or what a building should reflect. The great modernist architects of the twentieth century—Le Corbusier, Mies van der Rohe, Erich Mendelsohn—reveled in ignoring it, snapping the bonds to the past. Rather, they felt their role was to impose their vision on the world, and they did that brilliantly, if not always successfully. A Mies building is a Mies building whether it is built in Berlin or Havana. This earlier generation of architects—like those who now try to follow in their footsteps—felt that the true architectural spirit is an authoritarian spirit. It is elitist. But after the disastrous movements of the twentieth century, how can anyone embrace any ism—be it modernism, authoritarianism, totalitarianism, communism, or fundamentalism? Architecture is not, and should not be, about labels. What is called for in the twenty-first century is a new philosophy for architecture, one based on democratic ideals.

And that is something I understood viscerally when I went down into the pit at Ground Zero with Nina; when I touched the slurry wall and placed my hand on its cool, rough face, it conveyed a text for what I had to do. In his *Confessions*, Saint Augustine tells of being in a state of despair. Then he hears a child's singsong voice. He doesn't know whether it is in his mind or real, but the voice keeps saying, "Take it and read it. Take it and read it." He interprets this as a divine command, and walks over to where he has left a book of scripture, opens it, and reads. He is filled with the light of confidence, and the shadows of his doubt disappear.

I don't claim that touching the slurry wall prompted a spiritual epiphany, but it was a revelatory experience, because in that moment I could read the wall, and I understood its message. That's what I called the office in Berlin to say. The slurry wall is an engineering marvel, a metaphoric and a literal stay against chaos and destruction. In refusing to fall, it seemed to attest, perhaps as eloquently as the Constitution, to the unshakable foundations of democracy and the value of human life and liberty.

This is the story the new design would have to tell. To a generation steeped in fashionable irony, I'm sure much of this sounds hokey. But in the pit, I wasn't embarrassed by the nakedness of my emotions. And, later in mid-December, standing before the families of the victims of 9/11, only an unprincipled fool would be embarrassed by the nakedness of emotion—mine or anyone else's.

In the weeks leading up to the mid-December deadline, when all the competitors would unveil their plans, the intensity of interest in the competition was overwhelming, electrifying. Everywhere I went, people accosted me to tell me what they believed should be built—or not built. If I gave a lecture at a university, no one asked about anything else. At my nephew's wedding, guests pulled up chairs at the reception and sketched ideas for me on napkins. The competition rules prohibited us from contacting the Families directly, but people everywhere acted as their emissaries. "Make it soar," they'd say. "And make it so no one can ever forget."

I became haunted by a verse by Emily Dickinson, one of my favorite poets:

> To fill a Gap
> Insert the Thing that caused it—
> Block it up
> With Other—and 'twill yawn the more—
> You cannot solder an Abyss
> With Air.

For the first time since high school, I studied the Declaration of Independence and the Constitution. I marveled at the language and the radical clarity of the thinking. I sat up late reading, and thinking about liberty and freedom and the values we hold so dear and, yes, self-evident.

The deadline came quickly, and on December 18, in an intensely emotional three-and-a-half-hour press conference at the Winter Garden of the World Financial Center, across West Street from the site, the architects presented their plans to a packed room. Television cameras covered the event live around the world. In the front rows were officials and politicians, behind them the Families, and then the press. The emotional intensity was such that Nina could hardly bear to sit in front with me.

All the entries were ambitious. Norman Foster had designed two spectacular crystalline towers, 1,700 feet high, which were said to "split and kiss and touch and become one" at three points, forming one megabuilding. Meier, Eisenman, Gwathmey, and Holl revealed a monstrous modernist grid—five identical 1,111-foot towers crisscrossed by horizontal sections. It reminded some of an iconic piece of the gridlike structure left standing after the towers fell. But most people thought that it resembled a giant tic-tac-toe board, dropped on the narrow streets of downtown Manhattan. SOM's plan was much like what I'd seen in Venice, and I wasn't taken with it then—or now. And the THINK team, led by Rafael Viñoly, actually put forward three separate schemes, one of which covered thirteen of the sixteen acres with a glass roof, which struck me a bit as an architect's ego run amok ("We can leave our mark on *all* of it"), and another that consisted of two huge latticework structures that stuck up into the sky like skeletons of the buildings that had stood before. I was astonished by the obvious advantage involved in presenting *three* different schemes, and immediately felt uneasy about Viñoly and who might be promoting him; the fact that he strutted before the audience with no less than four pairs of eyeglasses affixed to his person—one on his nose, one on his forehead, one hung around his neck, and one in his shirt pocket—did not inspire confidence either. But I was impressed by the cathedral-like beauty of United Architects' buildings, despite their obvious impracticalities.

All the schemes were powerful and reflected strong senses of individuality. Yet interestingly, they all fired at the same target. They aimed to create an impressive high point, and ultimately to replace the Twin Towers. My plan differed in two fundamental respects. First, I focused down—into the bedrock, into the pit, because I felt that was where the memory of the site also resided, and not only in the development of high-rise buildings. Where the other architects referred to the towers that had existed before, I believed the goal was not to re-create the past, but to reinterpret it. Second, where the majority of the other architects presented ideas for megastructures, my aim was to mold the site into a coherent and symbolic whole by designing buildings that would ascend gradually in a pattern. And I wanted not to build just another isolated building here, but to create a new neighborhood, a new harmonious community.

I was chosen to make the first presentation. Moments before we began, Alexander Garvin came over and said, "Mr. Libeskind, you understand that with this live feed you will be talking to two billion people around the world." Even if I was experienced at talking to crowds, that was not what I wanted to hear.

Rachel, who was only thirteen, turned to me and, stroking my back, said, "Don't worry. Just speak your thoughts, Papa." She reminded me so much of my mother at that moment. My mother used to say, "It's not a crowd, it's just a real person you're talking to." Two billion of them, but all right.

I told the room that I called my plan "Memory Foundations." I told them about what Nina and I had seen in the slurry wall and the bedrock. And I told them that down in the pit, I thought back to my family's arrival in New York Harbor, just offshore from here, and that the memory of looking up at the Statue of Liberty had inspired part of my design. I envisioned five towers—tall but not too tall—arranged by increasing height, from south to north, so that they rose in a spiral with the same shape as the flame in Lady Liberty's torch. And the tallest, I had decided, should rise to 1,776 feet, to commemorate the Declaration of Independence, which brought democracy into the modern world. I would fill the upper floors of the tower with botanical gardens, as a confirmation of life.

There would be a memorial site sinking into the bedrock of Manhattan and exposing the foundations of the World Trade Center, and a walkway along the slurry wall. Sheltering it, in an embrace, would be a museum and other cultural buildings. I wanted to remember the heroes of that day, and I'd traced on a map the routes taken by rescue workers, police, and firefighters to arrive at the towers. I incorporated those lines into the design, turning them into pathways shooting out into the city from a public space at the intersection of Fulton and Greenwich streets, which I called September 11 Plaza.

I imagined an even greater plaza, a triangular area that would become lower Manhattan's largest public space. I called it "The Wedge of Light," and it was inspired by the ray of sunlight that had made its way down to us as we toured the bathtub back in October. The plaza, which would connect the World Trade Center site to the Hudson in the west and Wall Street in the east, would be defined by two lines. The first would be a line of light that strikes on September 11 of every year at precisely 8:46 a.m.—the moment when the first jet smashed into the North Tower. The second line would mark the spot where, at 10:28 a.m., the second tower buckled into dust and debris. These two moments of that day would define the Wedge of Light, which would commemorate the events of that unforgettable morning.

As I walked the audience through the steps of my scheme, I could feel their eyes bore into me. There was a moment of silence when I finished. And then the applause began, at first slowly, I think, but it grew in percussive waves, and when I focused on the faces of the people in the crowd, many of whom were now standing, I saw that many were crying.

By listening to my own experience, I had sought the notes to strike a chord that could resonate widely: I had tried to find the words and the images that articulated the feelings that lay in so many hearts. And in doing so I had envisioned a plan that would embrace the meaning of the place.

My proposal had "struck a common nerve," the critic Ada Louise Huxtable wrote in *The Wall Street Journal*. "One had the sense, at the presentation, of an end to an undefined yearning and search. You could tell by the sustained applause and tears that this is what people really wanted, and what New York needs. . . . Forget the additional time and expense of a competition, nothing will ever be better than this."

When the press conference was over, Nina and I were surrounded by family members of the victims. A wonderful woman named Nikki Stern, who had lost her husband, came up to us. "You must understand," she said, "I lost everything in the attack. I had only him. I don't even have a goldfish." We became friends.

Christy Ferrer slipped her card into my pocket. Her stylish clothes belied the pain in her eyes. She had not been married very long to Neil Levin, who was breakfasting at Windows on the World on the morning the planes struck. He had only recently been appointed executive director of the

Port Authority. I pulled the card out later to find that it read simply: "I just heard you speak. Please call me." I did, and we have stayed in touch since.

Two remarkable men, Lee Ielpi and Jack Lynch, approached Nina and me. Both had lost sons, New York City firemen, on 9/11; Jack himself is a retired fireman. Their handsome faces were etched with unspeakable grief, and they carried with them a roll of glossy white paper. "We'd like to show you something," they said. They took us aside and carefully unrolled the paper. The sheet, almost a yard long, was an indecipherable pointillist canvas, a dense sea of red dots.

"Do you know what this is?" they asked.

We stared at them blankly.

"This is the mapping of all the bodies—and body parts—found on the site."

My eyes snapped shut. There must have been ten thousand dots, maybe more. I heard Nina call out, "Oh, Daniel," and it felt as if each dot were exploding in my heart.

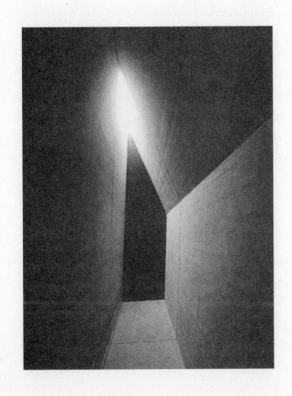

After the Winter Garden presentations, another man, whose name I never learned, came up to me. He said, "I can't believe you thought of the Wedge of Light. My wife was on the hundred-fourth floor of Tower One, and I'm fairly certain she jumped. I want to believe, Mr. Libeskind"—and here he broke into tears—"I want to believe that the last thing she saw was sunlight."

What an extraordinarily strange, powerful thing light is. Rays filled with hope. How do you talk about light without talking about the divine? About something that lies beyond the human? About perfection? Le Corbusier famously asked, "What is architecture?" His answer, and I paraphrase, was that it's the perfectly proportioned harmony of forms in light. But what does this mean? In essence, it means that perfection lies beyond anything we can think of. It's almost a point of view from beyond, from God's perspective.

Maybe I think this way because I am an architect, but light becomes tangible only when it lands on something solid—a body or a building—when it crawls, darts, engraves its presence on a wall. A city reveals itself in the shadows that its buildings cast. What color is light? Whatever color it alights on.

Many years ago, when Nina and I were in our twenties, we traveled with a friend around Italy in search of ancient temples. We were lost, somewhere south of Naples. It was extremely late, and we were exhausted and broke, so we sank into chairs we found propped outside a closed-up sidewalk café, and fell asleep. A few hours later, I woke with the early-morning light, and when I focused my blurry eyes, there in front of me were the temples of Paestum, the great Temple of Poseidon and the Basilica, a luminous, golden pink in the dawn. Timeworn and broken, they rose into the light and stood in seeming defiance of gravity. The beauty was unsurpassable, almost paralyzing.

I realized I was seeing the temples from the same view from which the Venetian engraver Giovanni Battista Piranesi, one of the finest architectural draftsmen ever, sketched them some two hundred years before. And what the scholar and architect John Soane, another idol of mine, had come to see and sketch a little later. Soane was such a passionate and

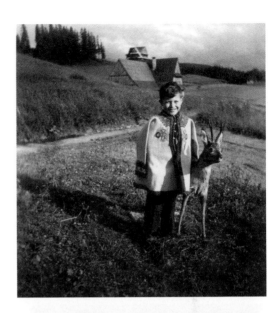

In the Polish countryside near Zakopane, 1954

My mother, Dora, and her store in Lodz, 1956

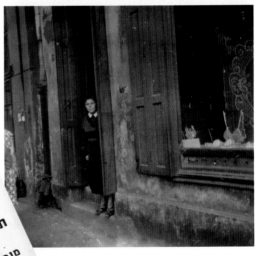

Ad for my mother's store, relocated to our new home in Tel Aviv in 1957

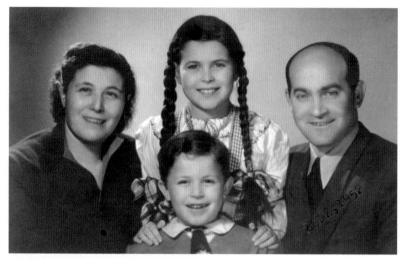

My mother Dora, my sister Ania, my father Nachman, and me, Poland, 1952

Reading a Yiddish newspaper,
Tel Aviv, 1958

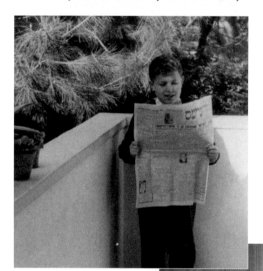

Winners of the America–
Israel Cultural Foundation
Prize, Tel Aviv, 1959.
Itzhak Perlman is on the
right, I am at left.

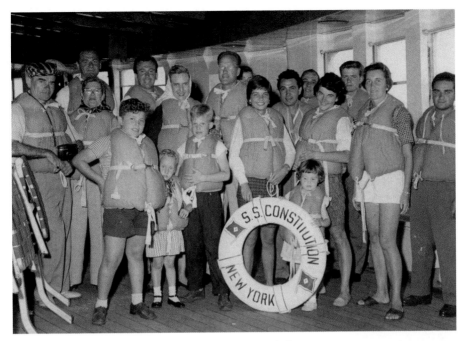

On my way to New York, August 1959. I am at front left.

I am a New Yorker,
the Bronx, 1967.

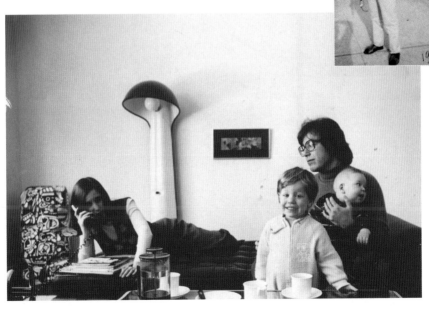

Nina taking care of business while I entertain Lev and Noam,
Cranbrook, Michigan, 1979

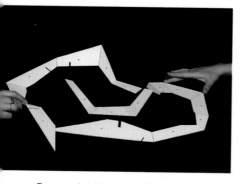 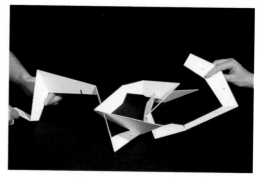

Denver Art Museum. "Two Lines Going for a Walk," folded paper model

Denver Art Museum.
Original watercolor
for competition

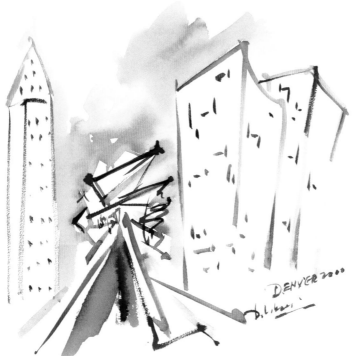

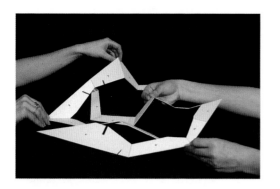
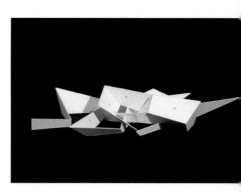

Denver Art Museum. Site model, wide view from civic park

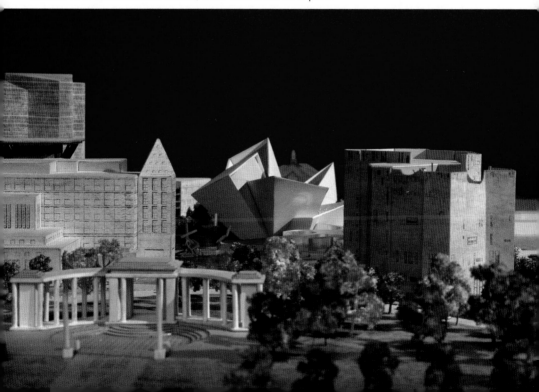

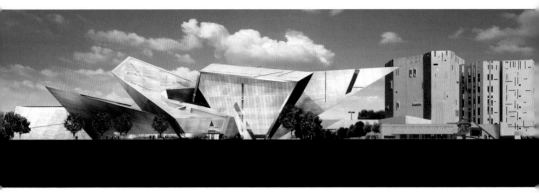

Denver Art Museum. East elevation rendering

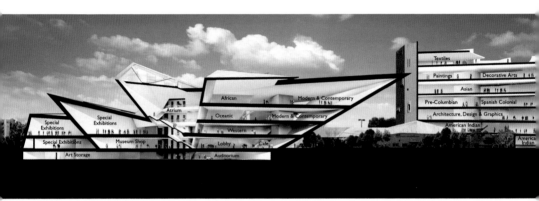

Denver Art Museum. North–south section

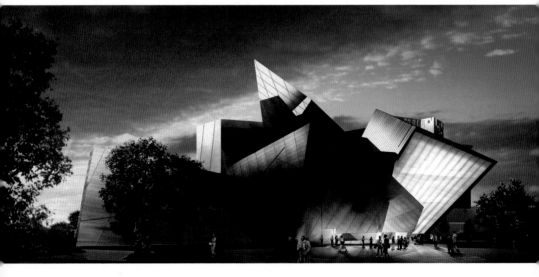

Denver Art Museum. Evening elevation rendering

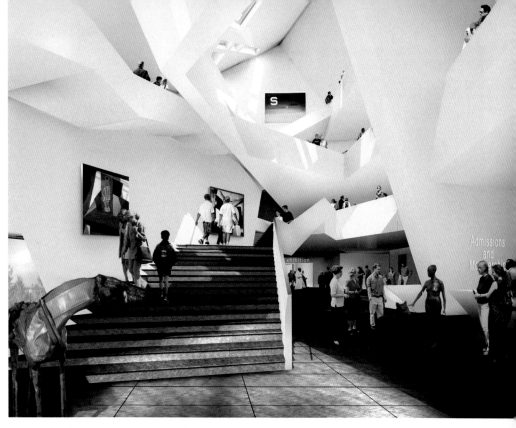

Denver Art Museum. Entrance atrium rendering

Denver Art
Museum.
Gallery rendering

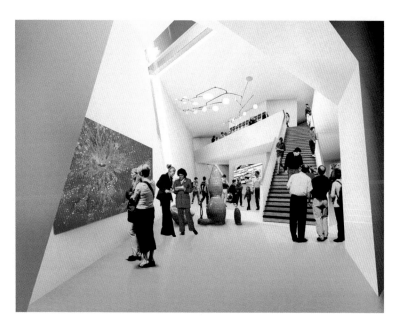

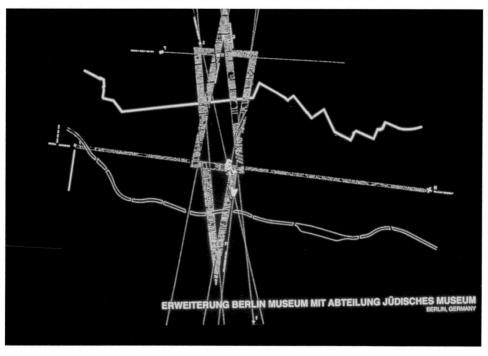

Jewish Museum Berlin. Star Matrix and Berlin Wall

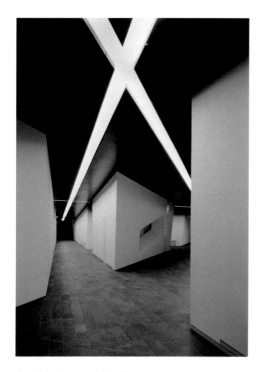

Jewish Museum Berlin.
Underground roads

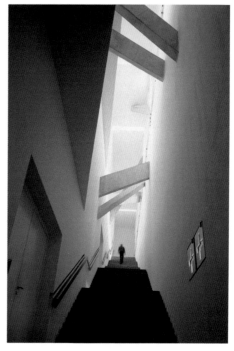

Jewish Museum Berlin.
Main staircase

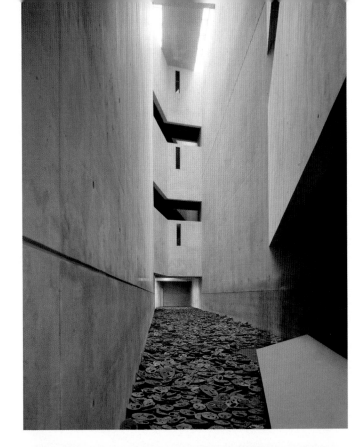

Jewish Museum Berlin.
Memory Void with
floor installation by
Menashe Kadishman

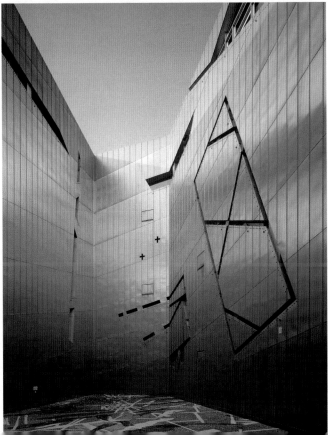

Jewish Museum Berlin.
Courtyard

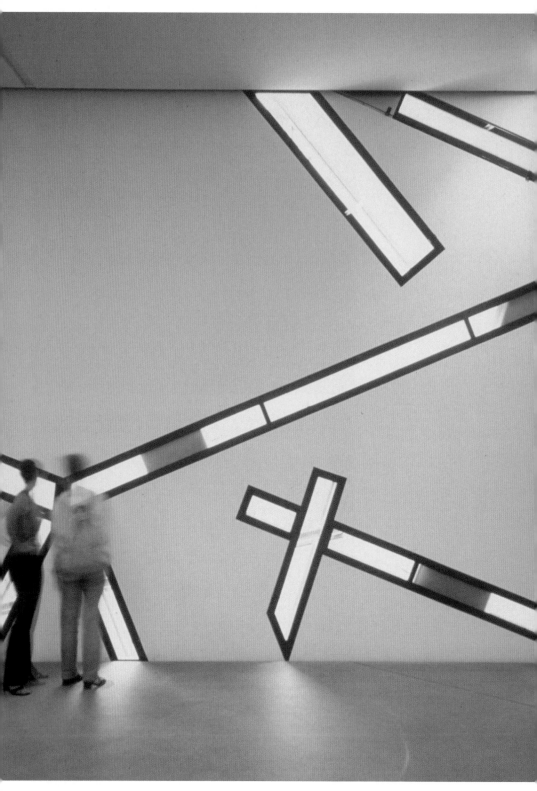

Jewish Museum Berlin. Exhibition space

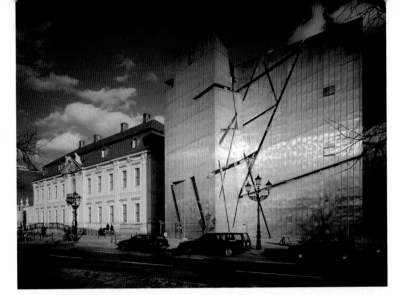

Jewish Museum Berlin. View of museum extension with Baroque building to the left

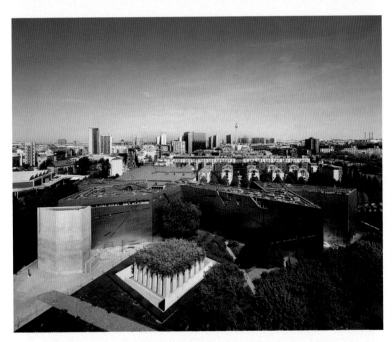

Jewish Museum Berlin. View with Holocaust Tower at left, Garden of Exile and Emigration in the foreground, and Alexanderplatz in the background

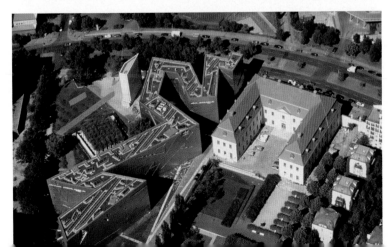

Jewish Museum Berlin. Aerial view

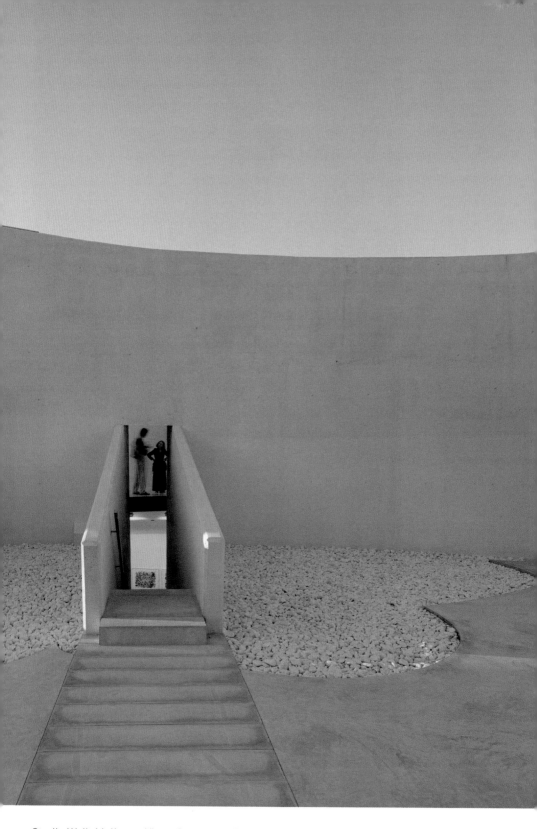

Studio Weil, Mallorca. View of entrance from sculpture court

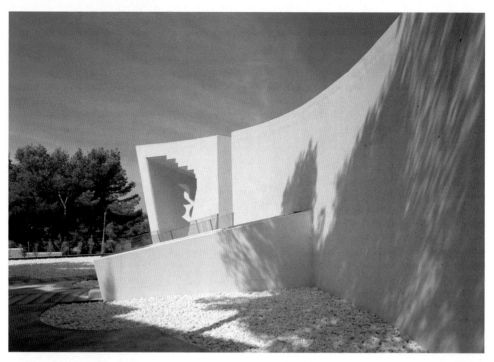

Studio Weil. Sculpture court

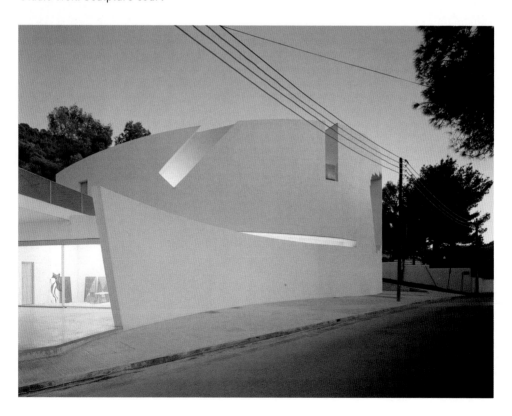

Studio Weil. View from street with studio entry

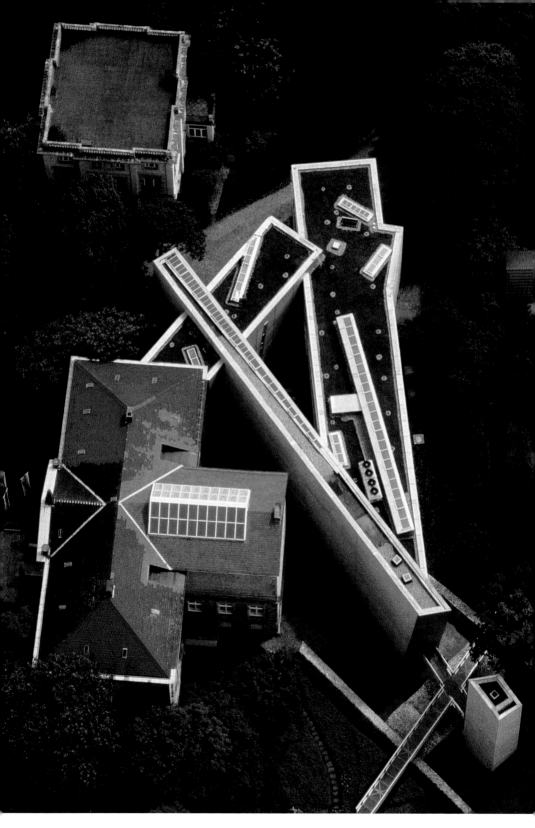

Felix Nussbaum Museum, Osnabrück. Aerial view

Felix Nussbaum
Museum. View
from courtyard

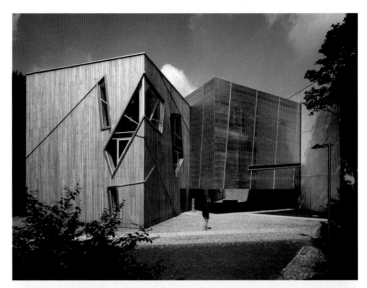

Felix Nussbaum
Museum. Night view

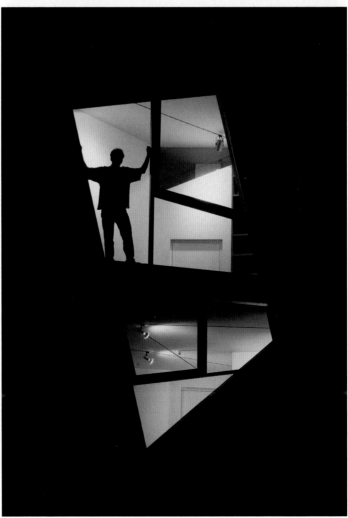

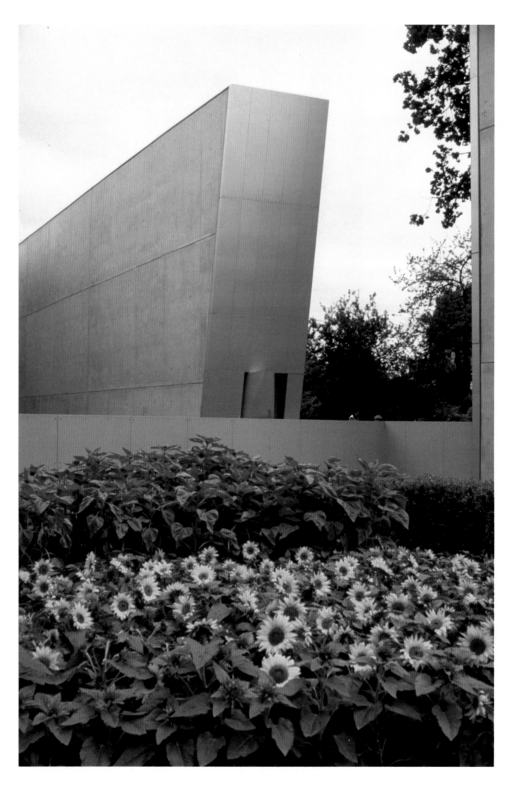

Felix Nussbaum Museum. Main entrance. Nussbaum's favorite flower blooms in front of the building.

eclectic collector of antiquities that after he died, a museum was made from the astonishing structure he had created at 13 Lincoln's Inn Fields in London. If you haven't been to the Sir John Soane's Museum, you must go.

Though the temples were now stately ruins, I could imagine what Piranesi and Soane had seen, and what the people of Paestum had seen in them more than *two thousand* years ago. I understood something I'd never understood before— that temples were venerated not just as architecture, but as gods in stone; lit up, they seemed filled with life, animated by ideas, ideals.

Light is divine.

When I designed the Jewish Museum in Berlin, I was tempted to build a room that had no light. The museum chronicles two thousand years of German Jewish history. Could there be one unsparing, pitch-black, hopeless volume in it to represent everything that was lost during the Holocaust? After all, there was no light in the gas chambers. I remembered a story told by a survivor in Yaffa Eliach's remarkable book *Hasidic Tales of the Holocaust*. The woman, who later lived in Brooklyn, recalled being transported by train to the Stutthof concentration camp, and just as she was abandoning all hope, she managed to catch a glimpse of sky through the slats of the boxcar. In the sky, a white line suddenly appeared, and she saw it as a sign that she would prevail. Through two horrific years in the camp, she clung to that sign as if it were proof that a miracle would occur and enable her to survive.

Only later did she realize that the white line might have been something simple and mundane, the trail of an airplane, the trace of a cloud. What matters is that it filled her with hope.

The significance of the woman's vision was obscure and enigmatic, and yet it had such a transforming power that I decided to incorporate it into the design of what I had come to call "The Holocaust Void." This is set apart from the rest of the museum, empty and forbidding, neither heated nor cooled. But it is not dark. High in the ceiling, and angled so acutely that you can't see it, is a slit that lets in a line of light, which is then reflected on the concrete walls and floor of the Void.

Light is the measure of everything. It is absolute, mathematical, physical, eternal. There is an absolute speed to it, you can't outrun it; that's what the theory of relativity is about. Stand here and remember what you can. What you remember is in light, the rest is in darkness, isn't it? The past fades to dark, and the future is unknown, just stars.

My earliest memories are all gray. Not because of age and distance; rather, gray is the color of the memories themselves— the angry gray of the cold northern European winter sky, the dusty gray of industrial Lodz, overlaid with the grayness of communism. That's the ultimate grayness—the grayness of everybody's being the same, doing the same thing, sharing similarly low horizons.

If you trust my childhood memories, there was no bright light in Lodz. I remember the grim courtyard of the turn-of-the-century building in which I grew up. To call it a courtyard is perhaps to give it too much credit. There was a space, there was a broken wall, and there was a wrought-iron pole that jutted out from it five feet above the ground. I always dreamed I'd see a man on horseback fly through the gates and magically leap over the pole. Instead, the women of the building threw their carpets on it and beat them so hard it's a wonder any dust survived.

I was one of very few children who lurked in the shadows of this courtyard. There was a little girl about my age with a white face and white hair who had bouts of somnambulism and sleepwalked around the courtyard during her afternoon nap. And there was a younger boy who had perpetual bubbles of snot dripping from his nostrils, so that in the gallery of mythical figures that is my childhood, he remains a feature-less creature with a wet face. But the courtyard wasn't really safe for a little Jewish boy. For that matter, Lodz wasn't safe for a little Jewish boy. Before World War II, there were more than 3,250,000 Jews in Poland. After the war, there were about 250,000, but in 1945 and 1946 there were pogroms—small but effective—and in successive waves, Jews either were forced out or fled the country. By 1950, when I was four, some

8,000 Jews remained in Warsaw, and only 5,000—compared with some 220,000 in 1939—in Lodz.

The only color I remember from those years was that of the huge bales of shimmering flesh-toned material in my mother's corset shop. They lay stacked about, like slabs of the tawny meat of an albino whale. My mother was expert in matching fabric to a woman's body. I would secretly watch from the back of the shop, and marvel at the distinctions she could detect in the tones of a client's skin. Today corset makers are more or less extinct, like blacksmiths or chimney-sweeps, but before the war theirs was a highly skilled endeavor and a valuable craft. And while most Polish women after the war had to settle for the appallingly ill-fitting mass-produced goods of the communist era, there were still enough actresses, and wives and mistresses of party officials, of infinitely varying shapes to keep my mother extremely busy creating perfectly fitting corsets, brassieres, girdles, and other items I didn't quite understand then and can't quite recall now. She put me to work inserting whalebone props into the finely sewn garments to give them structure. Long before architecture school, I had an education in applied Euclidean forms.

I can still see my mother's shop window. The sign is a woman's shapely hourglass figure, and in the window are three meticulously painted ceramic figurines. The first is fully dressed and stands with a parasol in hand; the second kneels gracefully in a corset, holding a rose; the third reclines sensuously, naked save for the miniature bra my mother has stitched. The display was too beautiful and colorful and my mother's entrepreneurial spirit too threatening for the Polish gendarmes to bear, and they hounded her, showing up at odd hours to inspect her documents and search for black-market goods, poking through her inventory, double-checking her accounts. No matter how they tried, though, they could never intimidate her.

I came home from school one day in 1957 and found small stacks of odd goods scattered around the living room. After years of trying to emigrate from Poland, my parents had finally received visas for Israel. The problem was that the zloty, Poland's currency, was worthless beyond the country's borders (within them too), so my parents had decided to take what little they owned, and invest in goods they might sell once we reached Israel. But there was another problem: What was there to buy? They purchased what they could—Bulgarian honey, raincoats and umbrellas, and a few precious sets of Silesian china, pink and white, rimmed with the thinnest gold. There were also a couple of pathetic East German motorized bicycles. These contraptions looked like bicycles, except for the tank hanging at the axle and connected by wires to the pedals. Pitiful!

All of our belongings fit into one relatively unimpressive crate. On our last night in Poland, I discovered I'd mistakenly left a valued notebook inside a box that was now tucked inside the crate, so I sneaked into the living room and, guided by moonlight, pried it open. In the dancing light, the objects glowed, a shadowy tableau of my childhood in Poland. There was something anxious, restless about them. These were precarious times. As run-down as our apartment was, it was sought-after, and we were watched constantly. The moment we left, others would slip right in and take over. Our leaving was dangerous. What if we were turned back at the border? Other Jews had made it there only to have their visas revoked without reason. If that happened, what would become of us?

The goods in the crate seemed to tremble in the moonlight. Or maybe it was just me.

The only person to see us off at the train station the next day was my music teacher, Mr. Sztajkowski. As the train pulled out of Lodz, we smiled our best Iron Curtain smiles—all surface, betraying nothing—but we braced ourselves for disaster. What if border guards decided to help themselves to the crate's contents? We dozed fitfully. We made it across the Polish border to Czechoslovakia. As we approached Prague, we began to feel the prison gates swing open, and the light filtering through the train windows was tangibly sweeter. We got past the Hungarian and Yugoslavian borders, where the guards patrolled with dogs; then we were riding over the bony hills of the Italian Dolomites, puffing through Trieste, sighing to a halt beyond the Iron Curtain.

Venezia. La Serenissima.

No soldier returning from foreign wars, no merchant returning from adventures in the East, could ever be as glad as we were to be in this city, yet we hardly had time to glance at the marvels around us because we were here to board the ship that would take us to Israel. My main memory of Venice then is not of cupolas or gondolas but of that damned crate balanced precariously on a tiny boat, maneuvering with difficulty through sepia-toned watery alleyways to reach the dock. What a spectacle we must have made, desperately clinging to the crate, looking like bent figures in a Francesco Guardi painting.

In Haifa we were met by my mother's family—a huge gathering of *halutzim* and survivors. Then we spent the first night at the house of Dora's half brother and his wife, but there was no tearful reunion. My uncle had been educated at Humboldt University in Berlin (a high honor for a Polish Jew), and he'd gained a Prussian reserve and a German wife. They were remarkable specimens of a broken world, these *yecker*, as my sister and I referred to them in whispers. (What a funny Yiddishism. *Yecker*, related to the German word for "jacket," was used by the poorer Polish Jews as a form of reverse snobbery against the more elite, and better-dressed, German Jews.) My aunt and uncle had been in Israel since they'd fled Hitler in the 1930s, but they still proudly saw themselves as Germans. They read German newspapers, went to cocktail parties with other German refugees, and perambulated—he in his elegant suit and homburg, she in her plumed hat—as if strolling the Kurfürstendamm in winter rather than Haifa under the palms.

They'd done their best to re-create a typical bourgeois

Berlin living room circa 1930—think *The Blue Angel:* thick drapes, heavy furniture, dark wallpaper, carpet underfoot, tchotchkes galore, dense volumes of German literature and philosophy lining baroque bookcases. But pull those thick drapes aside, and you were greeted by the brightness of the Mediterranean sky. My aunt and uncle had procured the requisite deer's head, which they kept stuffed and mounted on the wall. It wasn't the traditional German *Hirsch* or reindeer, but it was close: a desert ibex.

It was into this lost world that we dragged our crate. My uncle rolled up the Persians, and we cracked its formidable shell. Dust. The Silesian porcelain, wedged between our mattresses, had atomized, encrusting the mattresses with piercing shards. The other contents proved equally useless: the motorized bikes didn't work with the fuel available at Israeli gas stations, and there was no call for umbrellas or raincoats in perpetually sunny Israel. At least we had enough honey to eat every day for a year.

Within months, Ania had mastered Hebrew and was negotiating our lives in the new country. We loved Israel, my sister and I. There were endless revelations. Foods we'd never imagined. We weren't used to seeing Jews doing manual labor. Until the eighteenth and nineteenth centuries, most European cities had banned Jews from owning land or joining guilds, so they became merchants, lawyers, financiers. Here, though, Jews did everything: they were bricklayers, farmers, carpenters, and soldiers. They were even—to my mother's horror—*prostitutes.*

We hadn't known many Jews in Lodz, and those we knew were, like us, Ashkenazim from Eastern Europe; but now we lived among Jews from Yemen, Iran, Morocco. We felt closer to these other new immigrants, from Africa and Asia, who whispered their own taboo languages, than we did to the second- and third-generation sabras—the quasi-mythical term for Jews "native" to Israel.

We had never seen beauty like this. Even now, when I visit Israel, as others kiss the earth, I stand in awe of the light. Some days I suspect that's what people are really fighting over—not territory, but the light. I've been to countries at similar latitudes or longitudes—Morocco, say—but they don't share this light. It's unique. Maybe it's because this is where the continents come together. Or maybe the light is so rich here because the region is so rich with history and civilization, infused with the spirits of Abraham, Hammurabi, and Hatshepsut.

As I've grown older and traveled more, I've come to understand that one's experience of the sky is different wherever one goes. In Denver, the mile-high city, you feel as if you're on a precipice beyond which there is nothing. You're penetrating the atmosphere; the closeness of the sun and the brightness of the sky astonish. The sky over Berlin could not be more different. It's a swirling substance, composed of leaden and azure masses, thick with winds whipping across the Central European plain, unobstructed by mountains, on their speedy way to nowhere. In Israel, you are caught in a duel between the intense blue of the Mediterranean and the fiery blue of the sky. It's as if the sea god and the sky god were two huge, wide blue eyes, one light and orbicular, the other dark and flat, and they're staring at each other in amazement and delight.

I still love Tel Aviv, but in the 1950s it was sensational—utopian and poetic. The country was not even ten years old when we arrived, and everything was brand-new: crisp, white, modern. The Bauhaus buildings erected all over the city have now yellowed with age, and I don't know how they look inside, but they were glorious back then. How ironic that this movement, which never really worked in Germany, where it started, would find its true place in Israel. Here, the cornerstones of the Bauhaus philosophy—a spirit of collectivity, a social ideal of egalitarianism, a commitment to the future—made perfect sense, and part of that philosophy involved making the world a beautiful place to live. These buildings were as beautiful and as inspiring as anyone could dream of.

One day in Tel Aviv, while my parents looked for work, my sister and I decided to go to the beach. We were living in a rented apartment very close to the sea, and the sand and the light dancing off the Mediterranean called to us. Ania and I didn't know how to swim, but the lure of the water was irresistible, and we climbed into inner tubes we found lying on the beach and waded in. Bobbing with joy, we floated and talked, God knows for how long, until one of us became aware that we could no longer see the coast. We had no idea what to do. And then we saw that we were trapped in a whirlpool, which began to whip us around and around.

We shouted for help, but were too far out to be heard. And then, by very unlikely chance, we were spotted by someone, and a boat made it in time to carry us to safety. We might have just disappeared off the face of the earth that day, under the startlingly blue sky, no one knowing where we'd gone.

Part of the crushing misery of September 11, 2001, was the fact that the attacks happened on such a beautiful day. Again and again, when you talk with survivors and family members and New Yorkers who lived through it all, that fact is mentioned. The dissonance was terrible, as if the clear, sun-filled brightness of the day were somehow fraudulent. I am reminded of a scene in Camus's *The Stranger*: the protagonist's mother has died, and he realizes that here it is, the saddest day of his life, and yet the sky is blue. How can it be?

I remember leaving the hospital on the morning of December 28, 1980, after my brave mother had finally lost her battle with lymphosarcoma. I looked up and realized that this was the first sky I would see that she would not share with me.

Here's something that's important to understand about the mystery of light: Light is about letting the darkness be there. I'm not talking about light as a contrast to darkness. What the builders of temples and cathedrals always understood is that some things should be left in the recesses of light, in darkness. The great artisans who built cathedrals knew that the light from candles would take the eyes only so far. From below we would never be able to see all that exists up above, but that didn't keep them from meticulously carving every angel. Besides, those angels weren't necessarily for us to see—they were for the higher powers. And even though the carvings might not be there specifically for us, we are aware of them; they speak to us with their very presence. That's part of their mission, in the same way, say, that the first bars of Mozart's *Requiem* have a mission. The sound is alarming, the chords are disturbing, and a mood is struck instantly. That's what great buildings do. From the moment you walk in, a specific mood is struck. The space has been structured, like a piece of music, with a certain voice and tonality.

Enter the great halls of Versailles, and as you approach the center, you're no longer just walking around a big room, you feel different. My first visit to a cathedral, at the age of ten, completely transformed me. It was in Poland, in Kraków. I walked out a different person, awestruck by the force of what was possible for people to build. As an architecture student, I studied Chartres cathedral; I knew all about it—the central tympanum of the façade, the triple-portal arrangement, the four-part vaulting, the thickness of the buttresses, the *piliers cantonnés*. And then I actually saw it, and all the information in my head vanished, because those facts were beside the point. What intoxicated me were those chords of light. Color tends to be abstract, but here, because of the stained glass, you could almost touch it. The coral and red fall on the columns, and on the floor. You want to pick them up. Light transforms color into substance.

Every cathedral has its own power to transform. San Giorgio Maggiore in Venice, a Palladio church, differs entirely from Chartres. It is pure, clear, and in a way that resists analysis, almost transparent.

Like music, architecture is often about direct encounter rather than analysis. If you are interested in a piece of music, you can analyze it after you've heard it, take apart its structure, explore its modalities, tonalities. But first you have to simply let it wash over you. Buildings often exert their magic, their genius, in a similar way.

In Harold Bloom's opus on the Western canon, he wrestles with the question of what makes a book great. He concludes that it all comes down to *strangeness*. A great book always leaves a strange impression, and if it's strange, it will remain strange, no matter how many times you've read it. But what is the strangeness in architecture? It's not the strangeness of language or story, but a strangeness of *scale*. Look up at a great building, and you can't tell objectively how big it is, or what color it really is, or even what it's made of. No part of it is objectively measurable. It's all a mystery. A bad building is different. You can see that it's made of stone or metal; everything about it is obvious and readable.

There's a magic to a great building. Maybe it has to do with the way light falls on it; maybe it has to do with the acoustics, the sound of footsteps in its hallways. Some buildings take a long time to get to know, but still they make you want to make the effort. You can go to the Wailing Wall in Jerusalem so often that there should be nothing more for you to know, and yet it radiates an aura—for me, a red aura—that makes people need to keep returning to it. A Greek temple stands in Segesta, in Sicily. There are only ruins, you can walk through them, and yet it's not fully penetrable. And then there's the Mezquita in Córdoba, whose forest of interior columns is as awe-inspiring as the infinity of a landscape.

Parisians hated the Eiffel Tower when it was first built. It was ridiculed as an empty-headed thing, and yet in time it became the most beloved structure in Paris. This may be true for any great building that is artistic. It cannot immediately become part of everything, it cannot easily fit in, because if it did, that probably would mean it was just a repeat of what was already there. Frank Lloyd Wright's Guggenheim Museum wasn't successful when it first opened in New York, but it has become beloved. When they opened, and even before, the Twin Towers were extremely controversial, but in time they became beloved (to some, at least), because they became part of the place and part of the sky.

People tend to forget that skyscraper cities are only about a hundred years old; they are young and constantly evolving. As all cities of the world begin to merge into one bland cosmopolis, I have to ask: Is this really what people want?

At the beginning of every academic year, I used to ask my graduate students, "How many of you think you are immortal?" Of course, no one would be bold enough to raise a hand. And then I'd say, "Well, that's not good, because architects should think that they can be immortal—that their buildings will live beyond them, forever."

Today, when the cost of constructing a large building is calculated, what is also frequently factored in is what it will cost to tear it down. The building is just another consumer product, like any other. How long will a car hold out? How long before you toss away that hair dryer? With the attitude that nothing is permanent, that all can be replaced, comes the impression that all that matters is to create a false illusion. A fancy façade is all you need. If it's not visible, there's no point in spending money on it.

I think of that sometimes when I drive along West Street in Manhattan and look up into the two new Perry Street residential towers designed by Richard Meier (a third is going up nearby). These glass-and-aluminum-paneled towers have received plenty of attention, in part because they are Meier's first buildings in lower Manhattan, and in part because of their shocking transparency and minimalism. (And perhaps also because the apartments come with doorknobs that cost $1,000 each.) The developer boasts that the apartments, among the most expensive in New York, offer unobstructed panoramic views of Manhattan, the Hudson, and the New Jersey waterfront. This is obviously true. And so is the reverse: passersby, driving on the highway, strolling, or sailing, are also offered panoramic views, right into the apartments.

In fact, we're almost forced to act as voyeurs and stare inside. In a dense city that demands certain behavior from its citizens—a respect for others' privacy is key—these towers challenge us to break those codes.

Architecture is ultimately about what you desire a place to be. I'm not sure that most people desire a place to be a fishbowl, no matter how handsomely designed. Maybe not all things should be seen frontally. Maybe not everything should be in the light. Maybe some things should be left in dark recesses.

I toured the San Francisco Museum of Modern Art around the time it reopened in 1995. The new building had been designed by the Swiss architect Mario Botta, and the museum staff was eager to show off the trendy postmodern digs. I quickly realized there were two spaces here: the public spaces, and the private work spaces. The public spaces were marble, but just steps away, in the cordoned-off staff-only areas, the materials suddenly switched to the cheapest possible. The craftsmanship was shoddy. What was the point of investing time and energy and money here, the builders seemed to be saying—who will know? Well, no one, except for the people who work there. Imagine what it is like to work in a building where such a contemptuous attitude prevailed.

I think of the brutal, modernist notion that the architect and urban planner Ludwig Hilberseimer had for the city of the future. In a drawing of his, the city looks something like Chicago or Moscow, except that all the buildings are exactly the same, and human beings look like little mice, functional points moving along in a faceless, anonymous place. I feel this way as I walk past new, soulless buildings and realize there is nothing to look at besides my own reflection in the glass. Such buildings have lost their sense of civic generosity and their feel for the public gesture. When we imagine the Chrysler and Empire State buildings, we think of their glorious pinnacles, and the way those pinnacles speak to each other and to the buildings around them. Yet these two buildings also participate in public discourse on the street level, where their doorways welcome the public.

As I look out the window of my offices at Two Rector Street in lower Manhattan, I can see one hundred years of construction right here, and I am stunned by the beauty of the view. There's One Wall Street, where the stones in the façade are all gently curved. To the right is a fairly anonymous building which, on its uppermost floors, suddenly decides to turn into a temple, with a full colonnade carved into the exterior. How wonderful! To the left is an imaginative, whimsical building decorated with elaborate carvings. You can't see these things if you're in the buildings themselves, but you can see them from the street and from neighboring windows, and they all talk to one another, play off one another. A perfectly proportioned harmony of forms in light. This kind of public gesture—a gift to others—dates back to the Renaissance, if not before. The people who put up these buildings weren't looking to become famous, but they were building for the ages.

Do you want proof that there is immortality? I have always been taken by an argument posited by the philosopher and writer Henri Bergson, who won the Nobel Prize for literature in 1927 but, sadly, is not in vogue. Bergson was an interesting man, the French-born son of a Jewish musician from Poland and a Jewish Anglo-Irish mother. The Vichy government made it clear that he did not have to register as a Jew, but finally he decided he had to join the persecuted. It was a cold day when he waited to register, and he caught pneumonia, from which he died. Bergson believed that dreams are proof that there is immortality. Think of it, he said: Dreams are luminous, filled with light, and yet they happen without any optical, or measurable, light. They offer us a promise of eternity. I also have my own proof, which has followed me from Lodz. When I was seven years old, an aunt in Brazil sent me an extraordinary mounted butterfly, with phosphorescent wings of a deep indigo. It was one of the most beautiful things I had ever seen, and certainly one of the few objects of beauty we had in Lodz. In those wings that glowed with an almost radioactive light I could see everything I needed to know about Rio de Janeiro, about nature, cities, light, the afterlife, eternity.

Soon my family and I will move into our new loft in downtown Manhattan. When we take our boxes out of storage and unpack, the butterfly will tumble out from where it's been tucked away, and I'll study it all over again.

I'm eager to move; the renovation has taken a long time. When we first saw the space, it was a mess—virtually irredeemable, with a funny shape that had been chopped into rooms in a clumsy fashion. Nina was ready to walk out the door, but I sensed something.

"If you don't mind, I'd like to just sit here by this window for five minutes alone," I told her and the man showing us the space. They shrugged and left me in a chair by the windowsill.

When Nina returned, I announced, "This is the perfect apartment. Listen to it. It sounds right. Come sit here, get a feel for the light. The light is perfect here. I want to live with this light. We will be happy here."

· 4

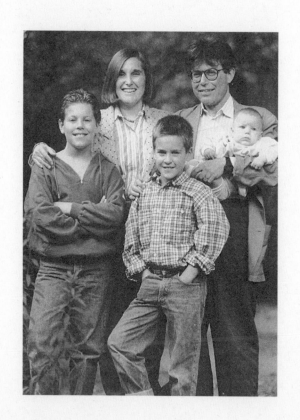

In 1990, with a contract for the commission
for the Berlin Jewish Museum signed, I stood
in front of an especially officious German border guard.

"Wie lange in Berlin?" he barked at us.

"How long?" I wasn't sure how long my family and I would be in Berlin. I was there to try
to get the museum off the ground, but whether
I'd succeed was uncertain. "I'm not sure exactly . . . not too long," I replied in English, and
then in Yiddish. He seemed to understand.

"Und was machen Sie in Berlin?"

What would I be doing? That was harder to
answer, so I pulled out the six-month-old letter from the Senate of Berlin congratulating
me on winning the competition to design a
"Jewish Department" for the Berlin Museum.
The guard read the letter with great delibera-

tion. I could see that he was mulling over his options. Was this good enough to grant us entry to the newly unified country? Normally, guards simply stamp passports with a visa and send visitors through. But this was no ordinary guard; meticulously he copied the letter into the pages of the passport.

I watched as he inscribed the words in German, in bold red ink: The architect Daniel Libeskind "is allowed to work in Germany for the planning and realization of the project of the Berlin Museum with the Jewish Museum."

"For the planning and realization . . ." The full implications of the words didn't hit me until much later, when it became evident that planning and realizing the museum would take far longer than I—or maybe anyone—could have imagined.

It began with a letter shoved into our mail slot in late November 1988. My family and I were living in Milan, where for three years I had run a happily iconoclastic alternative architecture program out of our home. I called it Architecture Intermundium (the latter term coined by Coleridge). Noam and Lev, then nine and eleven, were turning into regular *ragazzi*. And Nina, to our great delight, was pregnant with our daughter, Rachel.

There is a parable by Franz Kafka called "An Imperial Message," which is embedded in a longer story, "The Great Wall of China." In it, a dying emperor calls for a herald to deliver an urgent message to a humble subject who is far from the castle. The Kafkaesque twist is that the messenger becomes trapped among the crowds at the castle, and cannot possibly fight his way out to deliver the all-important words.

That's what it felt like when I opened the letter shoved in the mail slot. Within seconds I knew: This was a message sent directly to me. I was the humble subject, and the West Berlin Senate was Kafka's emperor. The Berlin government has always promoted cultural affairs, and now it was inviting me to participate in an architectural competition to create a Jüdische Abteilung—a Jewish Department—for the Berlin Museum.

Jüdische Abteilung! The words stabbed me in the heart.

On the face of it, the Senate's intention was admirable. It was indeed time for the Berlin Museum to acknowledge the incalculable cultural and historical contributions made by Jews. But to use that phrase! It was the *very phrase* used by Adolf Eichmann, the SS lieutenant colonel who masterminded the removal of Jews from their homes into ghettos, and from ghettos into the cattle cars that took them to the camps. It was the Jüdische Abteilung der Gestapo that had the responsibility for carrying out the "Final Solution" (a phrase Eichmann claimed to have coined).

The competition organizers weren't thinking much about history, I suppose. Or perhaps they hadn't moved very far *in* history. They were unable to imagine the Jews in any way other than as outsiders. As they saw it, there would be a sculpture department in the museum, and a film department, and a fashion department, and now there would be a Jewish department. But how can you separate the history of non-Jewish Berliners from the history of Jewish Berliners? You can't, any more than you can easily separate the molecules in a glass of water. They are, as Amos Elon put it, "two souls within a single body," sharing a tangled thousand-year history, and together creating what once seemed an enviably evolved culture. If Berlin had been a success as a city—and most agree that it had—it was because of the efforts of Gentiles and Jews alike. So it makes no sense to continue to treat Jews as outsiders, cordoning them off in a separate "department."

Then again, the city's Jews were never as fully integrated as they'd hoped to be. Even in the nineteenth century, a flourishing period for them, reality was scratchier than we might like to imagine. In *The Pity of It All*, his history of the German Jews, Elon writes about Rahel Levin Varnhagen, a brilliant and energetic Jewish woman who in the late eighteenth and early nineteenth centuries turned her home into a literary salon. But in an earlier portrait, *Rahel Varnhagen: The Life of a Jewess*, Hannah Arendt painted a far less comfortable picture of Varnhagen and the life she lived in Berlin. Quoting from her diaries and letters, Arendt focuses on the bitter regret Varnhagen suffered late in her life, when she realized that she'd never really been accepted by the Gentiles of Berlin, and was forced, on her deathbed, to face the fact that her attempts to assimilate had failed.

I thought all these things as I stood reading the letter from the Berlin Senate. "You are invited . . . The competition guidelines are as follows . . . The deadline is . . ." STOP. I had missed the deadline. The cutoff had been weeks before. The entrants were to report for a general briefing in Berlin the very next day at noon.

It was like a bad joke: The Germans had efficiently mailed the invitation two months earlier; the Italians had buried it in a post office somewhere, to release it only now, stamped IN RITARDO—late—in big red letters, as if that took care of matters. *Maledetta la posta!*

I called the organizers to beg for an extension, but they rebuked me for not following the rules. I sank morosely into a chair, stared into space. I don't know how long I sat there before Nina came home. "Well, we'll just have to get them to understand," she said.

"There's no point," I answered miserably. "They're intractable."

Nina plucked the letter from my hand and headed for the phone.

At 11:59 a.m. the next day, I stood at the Berlin Museum with the scores of other candidates for our initial briefing.

I'd never built a building before. Nina has always said that I was a late bloomer, which is true: it wasn't until I was in my fifties that a building I'd designed was built. I was an architectural theorist and an academic, but most of all I explored architecture through drawing. I had been more interested in ideas and abstract concepts than in the utilitarian aspects of the field. The only competition I'd won was in 1987, for housing designed for West Berlin. I called it "City Edge," and it was an attempt to rethink scale and form for a divided city. It was a kind of skyscraper, neither vertical nor horizontal, rising from the ground so that it would float out above the city streets and look over the Wall. Then the Wall fell, the land changed hands, and the project was scrapped.

But now, the letter from the Berlin Senate felt like a personal message, a challenge of enormous dimension. I was inspired to create a design that would take on the central idea underlying the competition. The requirement was for a separate extension for the Berlin Museum that would house various departments; I would offer a design that would architecturally integrate Jewish history into Berlin's rich, multi-textured history and enable people, even encourage them, to feel what had happened.

I showed my design to two friends, both fine architects, before I submitted it. "Daniel," they said, "you'll never win! You've broken too many rules. They will disqualify you."

But I've never followed rules I don't believe in, and I couldn't start following them now.

The philosopher Theodor Adorno said that anyone who takes a neutral view of the Holocaust, who is able and willing to discuss it in statistical terms, is taking the position of the Nazis. It's a radical statement, but I think he was basically right. If, in architecture, you neutralize the issue, if you find yourself focusing on numbers and "good taste," then you are no longer participating in the truth of it.

But then what do you do? You struggle to find the most immediate way to get at the truth. What was needed, as I saw it, was a building that, using the language of architecture, speaking from its stones, could take us all, Jews and non-Jews alike, to the crossroads of history, and show us that when the Jews were exiled from Berlin, at that moment, Berlin was exiled from its past, its present, and—until this tragic relationship is resolved—its future.

Architects from around the world had entered the competition. Almost all the entrants came up with a similar image: a neutral space, soothing and attractive, where one could visit the remains of a once flourishing culture after viewing other exhibits in the big Baroque building.

Here's what my proposed building would look like when it was finally built:

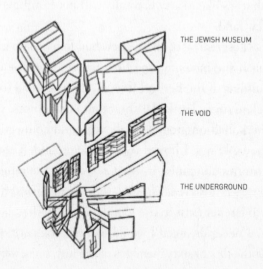

THE JEWISH MUSEUM

THE VOID

THE UNDERGROUND

Running through its zigzag form was a Void—a kind of cut in which there is nothing. The Void ran, straight but broken, through galleries, across passageways, into office spaces, and back out of them. The entire premise of the Jüdische Abteilung, I thought, was in that Void.

I had a passage that led to a dead end.

I had a space, the Holocaust Tower, that got so dark you couldn't see your feet, and the only light filtering down came from a slit in the roof that was barely visible from below.

I had a garden where the vegetation was out of reach, in forty-nine tall pillars overhead, and where the foundation was oddly tilted, making visitors feel disoriented, even seasick. The garden was to commemorate the Jews who had been forced to flee Berlin, and I wanted visitors to be reminded of the shipwreck of German Jewish history, reminded too of what it's like to arrive, totally without bearings, in a strange, new land.

Most radical of all, the new building had no front door. To reach the museum, one first had to enter the old Baroque building of the Berlin Museum, then descend to three roads below street level. All the other competitors, every one of them, had on-ground or aboveground connection between the buildings; I linked them underground. Though the two histories contained in their respective buildings might not always be visibly connected, they are inextricably bound, and will forever exist in the foundation of Berlin.

I never dreamed I would win the competition, yet I did. Of the fifty or sixty members of the jury, some were architects, but there were also government officials, members of Berlin's Jewish community, media and business people, and historians. It was a thrilling moment when I was selected. The jury recognized that my plan was neither dogmatic nor glib; that it served as an individualized mirror, which each visitor could read in a different way. They valued its authenticity and celebrated its originality. I felt honored and elated.

Of course, the building still had its detractors.

"*Unmöglich! Unmöglich!*" I'd hear them mutter as they studied the model. "Impossible! It is structurally impossible, it cannot be built." But I knew it could be.

"Well, if it's built," they said, "it won't really be able to stand up, or be walked through."

That's nonsense, I said.

"Well, if it stands up, it can't have exhibitions in it. If it has exhibitions, the exhibitions won't work."

They'll work.

"But where do things go? Where do you put the Prussian weapons used by Jews? Where do you put the Jewish soldiers who died in World War One?"

That was a good question. It's hard to separate histories.

In the summer of 1989, the Libeskind family's future was looking sunny. Three years earlier we'd taken a gamble and left the Cranbrook Academy of Art in Michigan, where I was head of the architecture department, for the unknown in Italy. At the time, our departure seemed impetuous and crazy, but living in Milan had paid off. And we'd won the competition for the Jewish Museum commission. Architecture Intermundium had been a splendid experiment; we'd attracted students from around the globe. Now I had received a spectacularly enticing offer: I jumped at the chance to be a resident senior scholar at the Getty Center in Los Angeles, a plum job that came with assistants, offices, housing, unlimited paid travel, and a regular salary. As the people at the Getty had explained, "Let's say one day you think, 'I'm interested in the Kremlin.' Well, then, we'll book you a flight to Moscow." Nirvana! We said yes. They found us a home with a view of the ocean; soon we were loading our belongings onto a ship headed for a warehouse in Long Beach.

All we had to do was stop off in Berlin to pick up the award for winning the museum competition, and we'd be on our way. We loaded the boys and the baby into a large taxi, bid Milan farewell, and headed to the Alps for a brief break. Then we boarded a train for Berlin.

It was July 4. As we stood stoically in the damp morning air on the border between East and West Berlin, watching guards take apart our compartment, searching for stowaways, I told Nina, "Oh, L.A. is going to be *very* nice."

Our first meeting in Berlin was with a senior Building Administration official. He took out a copy of my plan, laid a piece of paper on top, handed me a pen, and ordered, "Okay, draw me the basement." He was setting a trap, and I knew it. Had I drawn an intricate zigzag basement to conform to the shape of the museum, he would have been able to discredit me. It would have been prohibitively expensive and difficult to dig such an underground. Instead I drew a large rectangle. Herr Dietz's face remained impassive as I slid my sketch before him, but I knew I had just passed the first of many tests.

Nina and I went to see Josef Kleihues, the prominent architect who had headed the jury. His office was gigantic, awe-inducing; it had once been the Sanitation Department for the city of Berlin. As we sipped tea in commanding armchairs, Kleihues congratulated me on my position at the Getty and lectured us on how things would now proceed. "You know, Daniel," he said, "it is doubtful this building will ever be built. It will be very difficult to get it built. But if it does, don't worry, we'll have a local architect oversee it, and you can fly in once in a while to check on it. That's how everybody does it. If I were you, I'd apply to do a small multiple dwelling, because those actually *do* get built." Nina and I nodded appreciatively.

Trying to cross Helmholtzstrasse to catch the bus back to our hotel, where the kids were waiting to be fed, Nina and I got trapped on a traffic divider. As we waited for the rapid stream of cars to ease up, Nina suddenly said, "Libeskind, you do realize what this means?"

"What?"

"If you want to get this building built, we can't leave Berlin."

"Are you crazy?" We were on our way to a sweet life in Los Angeles. A home with a view of the ocean, endless sun, a steady income. Besides, our belongings had been loaded onto a ship for the slow voyage to California.

"Well, I don't care either way," Nina said. "It's your decision. But if you want to build this building, we have to stay in Berlin."

What Nina had glimpsed between the lines of Kleihues's explanation was that, yes, the museum was a high-risk gamble with a very slim chance of success—yet there was a chance nonetheless.

I had been doing my own reading-between-the-lines lately: when people spoke about the building, their faces lit up, and they peppered me with questions. There might be resistance to building it, but people cared about it.

"I'll stay on one condition," I told Nina. "You work with me."

Now, Nina has had many careers. She has run political campaigns, headed international organizations, and worked as a labor arbitrator, but she knew little about architecture. That was all about to change. "Of course," she said, and we have worked as an inseparable team ever since.

When we arrived back at the hotel, the concierge asked how long we would be staying. "Until the building gets built," I answered. The concierge, who had been following the coverage in the papers, burst out laughing.

At that moment, standing on the divider on Helmholtz-strasse with Nina, I had a revelation. For the first time I truly understood: This wasn't only about making drawings and models and having a discourse. It was also about getting this building built. I had no previous experience. Imagine that you've been trained as a surgeon but you've never had your hand on a scalpel, and someone says, "Now you are going to operate on this head." Maybe that's not the right metaphor, but that's how it felt at the time. My life had been set in one direction, and now it was about to take a powerful new course.

Fine, we would stay in Berlin, but what would that entail? How were we to start? There wasn't even money for the building. Some money had been appropriated for the competition, but that was all. There was nothing to work with. It was like having someone gesture to you, and you think he's saying hello when in fact he's waving good-bye.

We were turning our lives upside down because of one ambiguous gesture. We needed to rent an apartment and an office, arrange to have our belongings shipped back from California, and find schools for the boys. The logistics were daunting.

We approached Deutsche Bank for a loan. The bank's headquarters was one of the tallest buildings in the area, and the view from the boardroom was magnificent. The city spread out in every direction, and you could see the Fernseh-turm, the TV tower at Alexanderplatz, pride and joy of East

Berlin. We were escorted to a long table, around which sat ten grave-looking men in suits. The president of the bank, Herr Misgeld (yes, that was his name—Mis*geld*), sat at one end, a stack of newspaper clippings about the museum in front of him. Mercifully, he spoke English; neither Nina nor I spoke German.

He complimented me on winning the commission. Then he asked: "What assets do you have as collateral?"

Assets? Collateral? I started to sweat. "We have books . . . a lot of them," I said. "Hardcover art books . . ."

Herr Misgeld looked at me quizzically. "And besides these books?" He seemed baffled as to why someone would come in asking for a loan of a quarter of a million marks—about $125,000—offering books as collateral.

"There's a Persian rug. But I think it's imitation—"

Nina kicked me, under the table. It hurt. She dove in. "The collateral is not the objects that we hold in our home," she said, "but rather will be tied to the contract we expect to receive from Building Administration for the museum construction."

Misgeld nodded, and then his gaze went to the grainy black-and-white images of the museum in the clippings before him. "Can it be *built*?"

I jumped in to make a case for the building. He interrupted me and turned to Nina. "Frau Libeskind," he said, "do you intend to make money on this project?"

And Nina said something very true, and also very clever.

She looked him straight in the eyes, and said, "We don't intend to fail."

I knew many addresses in Berlin. I knew them because so many were secretly woven into the plans for the project, which I called "Between the Lines, Jewish Museum, Berlin." When I'd started thinking about what to design, I'd bought a map of Berlin. Then I'd pulled out a dog-eared copy of my favorite book on the city, *Einbahnstrasse*, or *One-Way Street*, by the literary critic Walter Benjamin. It's a strange book, a supposed guidebook—marvelously enigmatic and apocalyptic, divided into sixty sections of aphorisms and ruminations. Benjamin was writing an epic reported to be his greatest work when he fled Berlin for France in 1933. Seven years later, unable to escape occupied France for Spain, and with his book still unfinished, he committed suicide to avoid capture by the Gestapo.

Next I'd written the West German government, asking for copies of the *Gedenkbuch*, or Memorial Book, which lists the names of all the German Jews murdered in the Holocaust. The entries, which identify many Libeskinds among the 160,000 Jews from Berlin, fill two huge volumes bound in gold-embossed black leather; also recorded are dates of birth, home cities, presumed dates of death, and the ghettos and concentration camps in which the victims perished.

I began plotting the Berlin addresses for names taken at random from the *Gedenkbuch* on my map of the city. (I found these addresses in prewar phone books.) Then I looked for the specific addresses of people I've admired, Jews and Gentiles, and I paired some of them, drawing a line from the address of one to the address of another. I "married" Rahel Levin Varnhagen to the innovative Lutheran theologian Friedrich Schleiermacher, a frequent guest at her salon; if you drew a line between their addresses, it crossed Lindenstrasse 14, where the Berlin Museum stands. Among other addresses I linked were those of the profound poet of the Holocaust Paul Celan and the architect Mies van der Rohe; and the fantasy and horror writer E. T. A. Hoffmann and the Romantic writer Friedrich von Kleist. When I had plotted six names and three pairings, I studied the shapes made in the process, and discovered that they formed a distorted Star of David over the map of Berlin.

When the museum was built, some people thought it looked like a broken Star of David. The building does fall on a corner of the star formed by my connecting lines. And if you stand on Lindenstrasse and look very carefully at the façade, you can see the traces of that star.

I then pulled out my double-record set of Arnold Schoenberg's unfinished opera *Moses und Aron*. Schoenberg was not only one of the greatest composers of all time, but also one of the finest thinkers of the twentieth century, and he represented everything splendid yet difficult about German Jewish culture. He was an assimilated Jew who, like so many others, converted to Christianity, less for religious reasons than for social ones. When the Nazis came to power, and he found he was no longer welcome in Berlin, he renounced his Protestantism and began to write *Moses und Aron*, celebrating the Jews in their liberation from Egypt. It was his last opera, and arguably his best, yet he couldn't finish it. Some say it's because he ran out of time and had to flee Germany, but I've always thought that he felt he'd reached the limit of music.

I decided that the museum I was designing would try to serve as the opera's third act. In its stone walls, in the final space of the Void, the characters of the opera would sing silently. And in the end, their voices would be heard through the echoing footsteps of the visitors.

It may seem unusual to base a building on an unwritten piece of music. Or on a guidebook that is not readily understood. It may seem abstract and inscrutable—and maybe it is. Yet this inscrutability is due to the absence of the people wiped out in the Holocaust who had a relationship to Berlin. And the relationship to that past provides the basis for understanding the new Berlin.

The competition organizers had asked for a report to accompany the models. I decided to do my report on musical notation paper (hence "Between the Lines"), but to write it with the structure of the *Gedenkbuch*. The exterior of the competition model was clad in a collage of copies of pages from the book, names of victims from Berlin—and named Berlin. Many Jews had proudly taken the name as their own when they'd moved from the countryside into the city; their deaths struck me as particularly tragic. I felt a significance in the six letters B-E-R-L-I-N, which one could use to form a six-pointed star.

On my drawings I inserted not only sayings from the Hebrew prophets, but also the names of Libeskinds—the name my grandfather Chaim had chosen for us. Chaim came from the poorest of Orthodox families, and it wasn't until he was an adult, living in Lodz with his wife and children, that he had to register in a census and declare a last name. Until then, like most other poor Jews from the countryside, he had been known by his patronymic, just as my father was known as Nachman ben Chaim—Nachman, son of Chaim. Forced to choose, my grandfather picked Libeskind, which had been his nickname—"lovely child." When he registered the name with the authorities, he deliberately left out the letter *e* from the German component *Liebe*, so that the name would not be confused with a German name but would be unmistakably Yiddish—*Libes*kind.

This was an anonymous competition, and had my name been discovered by any of the jurors, I would have been disqualified; but it blurred in with all the rest. The competitors were asked to select numbers with which to identify themselves. I chose 6,000,001.

I had always imagined the building as a sort of text, meant to be read, and it pleased me that the jurors, while they didn't spot my name on the model, nevertheless evidently read the intent of the project, the many layers of meaning. But it took me a while to understand that although they had been impressed by the plan, that didn't mean the jurors thought it could be built. In fact, I came to see that its complexity pleased many of them in part because it made it so unlikely to be built. If they had really wanted to construct a "Jewish Department," they would have opted for something more mundane and obvious. But here they could showcase their collective concern and bold spirit—and at the same time shrug away, with regrets, of course, the possibility of constructing anything. "Yes, it's a remarkable design, but impossible to build, you know."

My bookshelves are filled with architectural books of winning competition designs that have never seen the light of day. In fact, ninety-nine percent of the winners never make it past the planning stages. It is much easier to win a competition than it is to get the scheme built. Berlin and Ground Zero: many of the same issues arose in the Berlin competition and its aftermath that arose at Ground Zero. In New York, the organizers imagined that the competition for the World Trade Center reconstruction would result in a changeable design. Thus they announced a "Design Study," by which they meant they invited ideas and possibilities that could be mulled over and, perhaps, pooled into a final concept.

But what happened in New York was similar to what had happened in Berlin: The competition took on a life of its own. The public lobbied for various proposed buildings. They weren't interested in the abstract. They responded to particular designs and wanted them built. New Yorkers were eager to heal and rebuild. In Berlin, the building we designed was swept into a vortex of public events. The Wall had just fallen, Eastern Europe was being transformed, a new Germany was emerging. Change was palpable. And Berliners were visibly excited by the future and eager to move forward.

Sometime after arriving in Berlin, I heard that the American architect Steven Holl had been called there by the newly appointed senator of building, Wolfgang Nagel, and that Nagel would be holding a press conference about the American Memorial Library, which Holl had designed and which was about to be built. I decided to go see what was up.

There onstage stood a beaming Holl, in front of a model of his unusual, sculptural library. On one side of the architect was a translator, on the other the pugnacious-looking Senator Nagel. The German press jockeyed for position, waiting for the senator to begin. At the appointed hour, Nagel stepped to the microphone. "I am here to announce to the architect that his project is no longer the winner, and we are opening the competition to others," he said. Holl, not understanding German, smiled contentedly—until the translator leaned over and whispered in his ear.

A day or two later, I received a call from someone at the Berlin Senate. "Mr. Libeskind, Senator Nagel would like to reexamine your project and wants to see the other twelve projects that were the finalists."

"He's out of his mind!" I told Nina. "I won the competition months ago." We were sitting under the red-and-white table umbrellas of the Kranzler café, around the corner from the Building Administration offices. In a few minutes we would face the man—whose name, not inappropriately, means "nail" in German.

"Can he really choose another scheme," I asked, "one that has already been passed over?"

Nina comes from a family of Canadian politicians, and is adept at reading situations. I am a naif.

"Nagel's not interested in choosing any other scheme. He's just interested in canceling your project. Let's figure out what he might ask you, and prepare ourselves."

When we walked into the room, the entire hierarchy of the Berlin Senate's Building Administration, twenty people at least, turned and stared at us. These were the people who got the buildings built. They stood rigidly in groups waiting for the senator to arrive. He was due at seven p.m., but it wasn't until forty-five minutes later that he stormed into the room, surrounded by an entourage of journalists and aides. He came straight up to me. We stood nose to nose. He didn't even bother to unbutton his coat. It was obvious that he was going to get rid of me in a second.

"What qualifies you, Libeskind, to build in Berlin?" he demanded.

I was speechless. It was not a real question.

"What big buildings have you built before coming here?"

"Well, Senator, it's not about big buildings—"

He cut me off. "I said: What big buildings have you designed that qualify you to build this museum?"

It was easy to see what he was trying to do. I took a deep breath. "Senator, if you go only by what has happened in the past, Berlin will have no future."

He stopped. Something about "the past" made him pause. "Okay," he said, jerking his head toward a model of the building, "is this the project?"

I nodded.

He studied it. "How do I get into this building?"

"There is no door for you, Senator. For you, there is no entrance to this building."

The room froze.

"There is no door for you," I continued, "because there is no way into Jewish history and into Berlin's history by a traditional door. You have to follow a much more complex route to understand Jewish history in Berlin, and to understand the future of Berlin. You have to go back into the depth of Berlin's history, into its Baroque period, and therefore into the Baroque building first."

Nagel studied the model. His face softened, and he said, "Mr. Libeskind, I don't care about your past. I like your style.

I welcome you to build in Berlin." And then he shook my hand and left.

Nina asked the Senate officials if they could find some bottles of champagne—which they did, and which they popped. Nagel had been canceling projects right and left. Everyone was delighted to be working again.

A bottle of champagne slipped and shattered on the floor. "*Achtung! Achtung!*"

"It's fine!" said Nina, who for an eminently grounded woman can be surprisingly superstitious. "It's good luck."

With our loan, we were able to move to Bregenzer Strasse, just off the Ku'damm. Our apartment was on the top floor, our office on the first. At first the office consisted only of a couple of desks, some chairs, pegs on the wall, and Nina and me, and our secretary, Dagmar Quentin, who often did double duty by taking care of Rachel. Gradually the staff grew to six, then to eight. We hired young German architects. This felt right.

One day an elegantly dressed young man in rimless glasses walked into the office. "My name is Matthias Reese," he said. "I hear you are building the Jewish Museum. Can I work for you?"

"What is your work experience?" I asked him.

"Well, I've built a small building in western Germany," he

said. "But I want to work with you. This project is what I have to do, what I need to do."

I admired his passion. Nina looked him in the eyes, trusted what she saw there, and hired him on the spot.

Only years later did I understand how remarkable—and right—it was that Matthias joined us and eventually became the project architect. We were walking through the Sachsenhausen concentration camp, when we came upon the Gestapo dance hall. There, the prison guards used to kick back, lift a stein or two or many more of beer, after committing their atrocities.

Matthias turned pale and very grim. "My father probably danced in this hall," he said.

I'd had no idea that his father had been involved in the war; as I learned now, he had been a private in the Wehrmacht, assigned to Sachsenhausen. I said nothing—what could I say?—but I was deeply shocked, because this was my friend, a man who had lived in Israel and had worked with passion on the Jewish Museum. And here, in this ugly and scarred place, was the ghost of his father.

Thinking back to that moment at Sachsenhausen reminds me of a trip Nina and I took with the children. We were crossing the Alpine passes into southern Germany and got turned around. The Bavarian countryside was growing dark, and the map was in the back, so we pulled off the road to get it. As I climbed out of the van, I looked around to orient myself. We were in the middle of a vast, open space. Then, through the darkness, I saw a mammoth stone structure with an imposing wrought-iron gate. No sign identified it. It was like coming upon an ancient ruin, but the gate seemed familiar. I knew this place somehow. . . . Then it came to me: *This was the Nuremberg stadium.* This was where Hitler had staged his infamous mass rallies. This was the past I had come to Germany to face.

Too exhausted to press on that night, we pulled up to a little inn on the outskirts of town. The chef had long since gone home, but the boys and Rachel were starving and the elderly lady who greeted us was kind enough to offer them Wiener schnitzel. I studied the lines of her face, and realized she would have been a young woman when the Nazi rallies were held nearby. She may very well have been there.

I am not the first to say that the sins of the fathers cannot be held against the children, but I was reminded of Germany's past every day that I lived and worked in that country, on the Jewish Museum and on other buildings. There is a new and very different generation of Germans now; and in the 1990s, after the Wall fell, and as an old generation continued to die out, I felt the city of Berlin and the nation as a whole undergo a recognizable change. I could sense something positive on the horizon.

That said, there was a corner of me that remained wary—which is why, I think, in my twelve years in Berlin, I never spoke German, officially or in private. After spending twelve years in the city, I was no longer just a visitor or a tourist. But I never stopped feeling an inner resistance to the language, and although I had become in many ways a Berliner, I always represented a certain foreignness.

"How is your German coming along?" people would ask me.

"Not so good," I'd reply, "but my Yiddish is improving by the day."

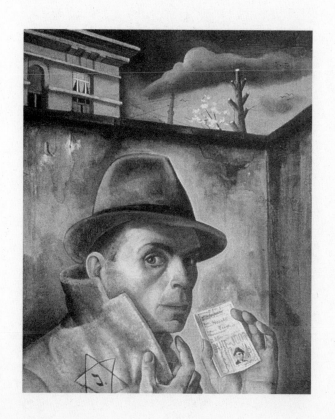

"So, Dad," one of my sons asked recently, "what did Mom look like when you first met her?"

The most beautiful face I've seen is Nina's, the first time I saw her at Hemshekh, a Yiddish camp in upstate New York, a last bastion of that lost world. I was twenty, and had come up from the Bronx to be an arts-and-crafts teacher; she was seventeen, and had come down from Canada to be a counselor. I was too shy to speak to her. I told my friend Jerzy, "She's so beautiful she must be stupid—no one can be blessed with looks like those *and* a sharp mind." That was one of those dumb things males said back in the 1960s and early 1970s. Or maybe I was just try-ing to protect my heart, because I knew immediately that I should be with her for the rest of my life.

"Nice story," my son replied. "But what did she look like?"

He wanted specifics. He wanted to know what

color her hair had been, whether she wore peasant dresses or miniskirts. If she was beautiful, what made her so. But there is no reason for beauty; there is no *because*. It just is. Beauty is the great mystery. And a face, well, it's really what you make of it, isn't it? It's the depth of a face that we respond to, not just the skin stretched over the skull. The word *face* comes from the Latin *facere*—to make, to do. What speaks to us is the way a face shines, not just under the sun but from an inner spirit and radiance as well.

We think we can remember the faces of those we've loved, but really we can't. I think I can remember my father's face, such a kind face, as he stood beaming on the pier, waiting for us to disembark from the *Constitution*. I think I can remember the faces of my children when I held them for the first time. I think I can remember Nina at camp. But I have to admit that the only way I can *really* see a face is to take its image from a photograph and commit it to memory. Yet that's simply a graphic image, not the true substance or impact of the face. After all, what is a photograph? Light exposed, chemically, on a plane, nothing more.

The living face is something entirely different. In the eighteenth century, and into the nineteenth, scientists studied physiognomy, with the intention of identifying and classifying human behavior based on the structure of a face, but of course their efforts failed. The fact is, when you regard a face, what you're really looking at is *what that face is looking at*. Think of your own face. You look at something, and even if it's inanimate, it looks back at you—and in that moment, there is some kind of communication in space, and your face responds to it and changes. So it is with buildings. They don't have just façades but faces that turn either toward us or away.

The great Argentinian writer Jorge Luis Borges had an idea that if you were to track all the steps a human being took from birth to death, you would be able to know the life that person led. I don't think Borges was right. You would never know what the person had beheld, where his gaze had drifted. Had he been surprised or delighted by unexpected sights? What spectacles brought light to his eyes? You need to know this in order to understand fully what kind of life a person has lived.

Not long ago, Nina and I flew to Denver to see the early stages of construction of my expansion to the art museum there. We drove straight from the airport to the construction site, and when Nina got out of the car and looked at the steel structure cantilevered way out over the street, she started to laugh. "Daniel!" she said. "It's wild!"

I said, "Thank God!"

It's going to be a terrifically unusual building, I think—a giant titanium-covered sculpture, rolling like a landscape, full of dramatic surprises.

Philip Johnson once said to me, "You know what architecture is? It's when I suddenly have this queasy feeling in my stomach and I say, *Wow*, it's pretty good." For me, it's not just about the wow, but also about the experience of dislocation, the shock to the system that comes from seeing something jarringly new or unexpected, so much so that you feel as if you have arrived in another place, between the known and the unknown.

The late Jennifer Moulton, who was director of city planning for Denver, was determined that the expansion of the art museum be a building unlike any other, one that would transport visitors into a new world. Denver already had a wonderfully original art museum, designed by the noted Italian architect Gio Ponti. Nearby was Michael Graves's public library. When the museum's director, Lewis Sharp, announced that an expansion was needed, and that it should be the first great art museum of the twenty-first century, Moulton rose to the challenge.

"Great design adds value to a city," she explained. "It adds psychic value, aesthetic value, and economic value, because it says you're a city that is moving, you're a city that is progressive, you're a city that has confidence in yourself. I think Denver's ready for it."

Oddly, perhaps, architecture is a field in which individuality is not well regarded. In art it is celebrated. In science it is demanded. In fact, success in most arenas is determined significantly by the degree to which someone can break from the pack and assert individuality of thought, dress, expression. Think of fashion designers such as Issey Miyake, Alexander McQueen, Vivienne Westwood. They extend frontiers precisely because they are original thinkers.

Imagine a world reduced to the same face, where everyone looked the same. What a nightmare.

I laugh about it now, but I wasn't especially amused when I was told why I wasn't getting the commission to build an extension for the Carnegie Science Center in Pittsburgh. Thanks a lot, the people said, but we're a little disappointed by your proposed design. Why? "We were hoping for a Libeskind-type building. This doesn't look enough like a Libeskind." They wanted an imitation of something I had already done! Why? What did that have to do with their building?

Unlike many in positions to commission buildings, Lewis Sharp in Denver is dedicated to architecture as an art form. He is backed by a smart and adventurous board of directors and trustees, in particular by a generous chairman, an oil tycoon named Frederic C. Hamilton. A thoughtful man with a keen sense of humor, Hamilton easily could have invested his $20 million in other ventures. Instead, because of his love of art, he chose to subsidize the museum expansion. His name will appear on the building when it is completed in 2006; he should be celebrated for his generosity.

When I began to design the expansion, I was inspired by many things—the light and geology of the Rockies, the industrial history of this railway town—but most of all by the wide-open faces of the people of Denver. I have a theory about that: Part of their exuberant glow must come from the way their eyes reflect that clear, high-above-sea-level light. Eyes are spheres; light bounces off them; they glisten and gleam.

Lewis Sharp gets that look, and he grew up on the Upper East Side of Manhattan, across the street from the Metropolitan Museum of Art, where he was curator of the American Wing in the 1980s. He told me he was six years old when he first crossed Fifth Avenue to enter the museum, and right then and there he decided, "This is it. I am going to spend the rest of my life in museums." And so he has.

I suspect that my father, who loved mountains, would have loved Denver and its optimists. He died in his nineties, having witnessed horrors most of us can't even bear to think about, and yet to the end he believed that people were basically good, and his preternaturally youthful and gentle face reflected this belief.

I doubt that my mother, who loved the sea, would have much liked the city, though. And with her sardonic take on the world, I don't think she would have fit in. She was brilliantly dyspeptic; what she'd learned of human nature all but depleted her faith in it. I can't write about faces without describing my mother's, one of the most mysterious I've ever seen. She had a perfectly curved nose, and sharp, high cheekbones over which peeked slanted eyes—two sentinels hiding behind turrets. Her tiny, fragile body—stunted by starvation, oppression, longings, regrets—concealed a titanic power that radiated from those eyes; they could freeze the sun or melt a glacier. When she moved to New York, people used to assume she was Puerto Rican or Greek. Certainly no one guessed she was a Hasidic Jew from Warsaw—or, as she claimed to be (and

I believe), a direct descendant of Prague's famed Rabbi Loew, conjurer of the Golem. My mother *did* have magical strength.

So fundamentally different were they in personality—my father outgoing and optimistic, my mother very private and wary—that I'm not sure my parents would have gotten together had their experiences during the war years not been eerily parallel, and had the world been a different place. But their wedding in 1942 in Soviet Asia sealed a love affair that lasted the rest of their lives.

Dora, one of eleven Blaustein siblings, was from Warsaw, which had the largest Jewish population of any European city. Nachman was one of five children of an illiterate, itinerant Yiddish storyteller from Lodz, which had the second-largest Jewish population. Both were smart, idealistic young Jews. My father was a socialist, a member of the Jewish labor Bund; my mother was a Zionist, and an anarchist, in spirit if not always by political affiliation. When the Nazis invaded Poland in 1939, Dora and Nachman both recognized that they would soon be targeted, so both fled to the Soviet Union; it would be three years before they met.

"Let me take your son Iser with me," my father begged his brother Natan, but Natan said no: "Whatever happens to one in this family will befall all." My uncle and every one of his children would die in the camps.

"Come with me," my father begged his sister Rózia, but she and her husband had just bought furniture for their budding family, so she refused. She survived Auschwitz, but she watched as her baby boy was thrown out of a window and her husband was shot. I say Rózia "survived," but in the years I knew her, she was a ghost walking among us.

Both my parents were captured by the Red Army and sent to hard-labor camps. The eight hundred men in my father's camp on the Volga were almost all Polish Jews; he did not see a woman for three years. My mother's camp, in Siberia, included women on Stalin's death list—the daughters, sisters, wives of party leaders who had fallen out of favor: the daughter of Stalin's former protégé Sergei Kirov; the sister of the theorist Nikolai Bukharin . . . The communist state was eating its own.

Only since the collapse of the Soviet Union has the full extent of the terror of the camps become clear. In her book *Gulag*, Anne Applebaum places the number of prisoners from 1929 to 1953 at 28.7 million. In 1940 alone, the year my parents were imprisoned, 1,659,992 people were sent to the gulags.

It was a brutal life. Subsisting on nothing but watery soup, bits of stale bread, and black water they called coffee, and dressed in cotton clothing and rubber shoes, Nachman and the other inmates walked for hours through snow to a work site, where, guarded by dogs and soldiers, they dug tunnels, built bridges, and crushed rocks, all for the "war effort." He always spoke of the absurd nature of this work—how one stick of dynamite could have dislodged more rock from the quarries than could all the prisoners together working for a year. But the absurdity was part of the strategy: the point was to keep the prisoners exhausted, dulled, unable to rise up. It worked. Unless the prisoner was my mother.

In a camp near Novosibirsk, Dora was put to work making leather boots and elaborately detailed shirts of the finest silk for the Soviet general staff. She herself wore only rags, and wrapped her feet in newspaper to ward off frostbite. The women in the camp were routinely abused by the guards—drunkenly beaten, and worse—and what injury the guards didn't inflict, lice did, boring into the women's skin and skulls until, in mad desperation, they scratched themselves bloody and raw.

One night, the camp's commanding officer rounded up some of the women and ordered them into his office. He screamed at them for being Poles, for being Jews and enemies of the state. Then he turned on Dora. "Whore," he called her. And my mother snapped. She seized an inkwell on his desk and hurled it at the portrait of Stalin above his head. The inkwell shattered, a thick stream of black splattering across the dictator's face and the officer's red rug. The women froze; the officer went white. But he didn't reach for his pistol. He didn't kill Dora.

Staring at my mother, he yelled, "Out, out! Everyone out—*now*."

Why didn't he kill her? Was it the shock? That vision of the ink-stained portrait is as indelible a memory of mine as if I'd actually been there. It is the very picture of the human spirit in defiance of tyranny. And it is the ultimate story of my mother's fearlessness.

It used to infuriate her that the phrase "Holocaust survivor" was limited to those who had survived the Gestapo-run
concentration camps. "They were the same," she'd say of the
Soviets. "They just weren't as efficient as the Germans, they
were slightly more primitive." Her cheeks would flush with
indignation.

My parents were set free in the summer of 1942—the result
of a deal struck between Stalin and the Polish government in
exile. But by then war had broken out between Germany and
the Soviet Union, and it was next to impossible for the newly
freed Poles to make it back home. Both of my parents had one
overriding dream, and that was to be *warm*. So Dora with her
friend Rachela, and Nachman with his friend Zimmerman,
began the slow trek south, hitching rides on a seemingly endless sequence of trains, until they found shelter in a refugee
center in Kyrgyzstan, a Soviet state surrounded by Kazakh-
stan, China, Tajikistan, and Uzbekistan. It was a world magically strange and unfamiliar.

One day Zimmerman announced to Nachman: "I met four
girls yesterday from Poland—they were freed from another
camp."

My father knew what to do. As he told my sister in his
Yiddish-inflected way many years later: "And I said, Let's go
out in the evening. So okay, we went out for the evening.

And we saw them. And Mama and me right away fell in love." Zimmerman met his future wife that night too.

The refugees, roughly fifty of them, almost all Bundists from Poland, were relocated to an Uzbek village, Uczkor Gan, on the edge of fields bright red with poppies cultivated for their seeds and for opium. The Kyrgyz Muslims were gentle and generous, taking the young Poles into their mud-brick huts and sharing with them what little they had. To the day they died, my parents never got over the sweet flexibility of the villagers—especially the fact that, in some cases, when the men went off to war, the women, though devout, adapted by living together as husbands and wives. This was something *not* seen in Poland.

A famine swept through the region. The mountains towering indifferently on the horizon were like a hallucination brought on by hunger. My parents survived by eating bugs and boiled weeds, mostly a form of nettles that irritated the skin and were painful to pick. My mother was impressed by an enterprising refugee who had gotten his hands on a bit of meat and for a few kopecks would "rent" it to others—dangling it by a string into a bowl of warm water for a few seconds to produce a pseudo-soup with a hint of taste. Nachman and Dora and their friends found work digging a canal and picking cotton, and for each day's labor they were paid four hard black nuts. This became the staple of their diet.

My mother's friend Rachela, who had fled Poland with her, and with her survived the gulag and the trek to Kyrgyzstan, succumbed to starvation. But my parents hung on, and even had a baby—my sister, Ania. My mother described Ania's birth amid that famine as a flower's blooming in the empty desert.

Two years later my mother discovered she was pregnant again. This time, she and my father decided, they would undertake the epic journey home. Sometimes they hitched rides on freight trains and horse-drawn wagons, other times they walked. From Tashkent, through the Fergana Canal, famous in Russian literature, to Moscow and Minsk, and on to Warsaw. Their only material possession was a sack of salt my father had dug out of a mine in Kyrgyzstan. It is said that in ancient times salt was as valuable as gold; so it was in times of war. Or so my parents prayed.

When they finally reached Poland, my mother was eight and a half months pregnant, and Ania was three. It was 1946, and my parents had been gone for almost seven years. They were unprepared for what they were to find. Sure, rumors had made it to Central Asia, but the picture was fuzzy, unfathomable. Much later, my mother would recount changing trains at the Polish railroad junction at Oświęcim—Auschwitz. The name meant nothing to her. She saw skeletal beings limping around, but she didn't think much of it at the time—after all, she had just survived a horrific famine and wasn't much more than a skeleton-with-child herself. Only later did she realize that she had been standing at the place where her family had been murdered.

Nachman stayed in Warsaw to sell the salt, and sent Dora and Ania ahead to his hometown, instructing them to look for his sister Rózia. But when Dora and Ania knocked at her door in Lodz, a sour-faced woman peeked out, announced, "She left yesterday," and slammed the door. Rózia had apparently gone to a displaced persons' camp set up by the Americans in western Germany. At least she was alive. Between them, my parents would discover that eighty-five of their immediate relatives had been exterminated. Parents, siblings, nieces, nephews, first cousins. All dead.

Dora, who was never one to cry, wandered the streets of the strange city sobbing. Mad with fear, Ania clung to her. Just when Dora had lost all hope, she came across a female Russian soldier by herself at a guardhouse. The woman looked like an ogress, my mother said, and her menacing Kalashnikov terrified her. But between sobs, and in broken Russian, Dora implored her for help. My sister, though she was so young at the time, remembers the incident vividly. The guard was huge, fat and big-breasted, with a gigantic head and even more gigantic boots; plumes of smoke from a clay pipe curled out of her nostrils. But this ogress had a kind heart, and she let Dora and Ania sleep overnight on the metal cot in the guardhouse. The next morning my mother went into labor, and was rushed to the hospital for refugees. There I was born.

Look at the face in the portrait at the beginning of this chapter. Look at those haunted eyes. They tell you all you can bear to know. This was Felix Nussbaum. Once he was considered

an important painter; in 1933 he received a prestigious German prize to study in Rome. But he was, as you can see here,
a Jew. He was imprisoned, but he escaped and hid, spending
many of those grotesque years in a tiny attic in Brussels, painting self-portraits that eloquently told what was happening—
to him, to the world.

"If you find my paintings," he wrote, "consider them to be
messages in a bottle tossed into the ocean."

He thought he would survive. But the smell of turpentine
and paint gave him away, and a neighbor turned him in to the
Gestapo. Nussbaum and his wife, Felka Platek, who was also
a painter, were eventually put on a deportation train to
Auschwitz. They did not make it back.

For a long time, Felix Nussbaum was forgotten. Even his
name was erased. During the final war years, his signature
was removed from most of his paintings, and they were sold
as anonymous art.

I had never heard of him, until 1989, when my family and
I moved to our apartment on Bregenzer Strasse in Berlin.
One day, strolling alongside the park around the corner from
our flat, I noticed a plaque on the façade of a building: Here
lived a painter, it read, who perished in 1944. Nussbaum. The
name meant nothing to me. When I got home I looked it up
in the *Encyclopedia Judaica,* but he wasn't listed in the 1976
edition. (He is listed in later editions.)

Almost fifty years after his murder, people in Nussbaum's
hometown—provincial, out-of-the-way Osnabrück, Germany,
not far from the Dutch border—tracked down some of his

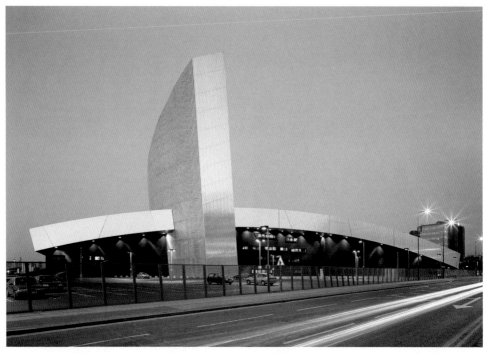

Imperial War Museum North, Manchester, England. Entrance from Trafford Wharf Road

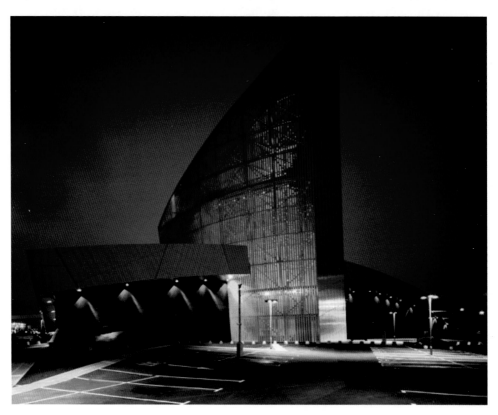

Imperial War Museum North. Night view

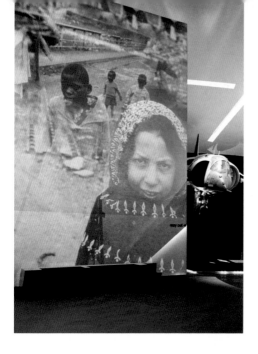

Imperial War Museum North.
Exhibition space with slide projection
and Harrier fighter jet

Imperial War Museum North.
Original concept sketch

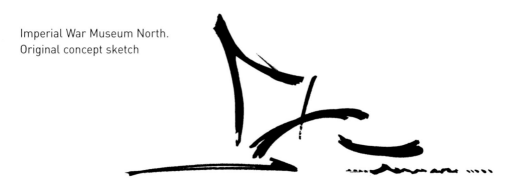

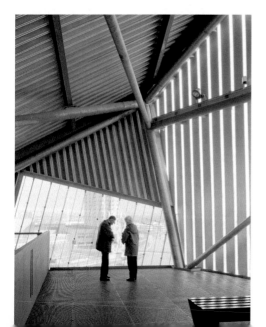

Imperial War Museum North.
Air shard viewing platform

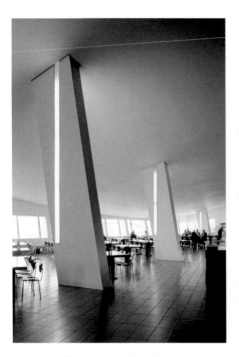

Imperial War Museum North.
Restaurant

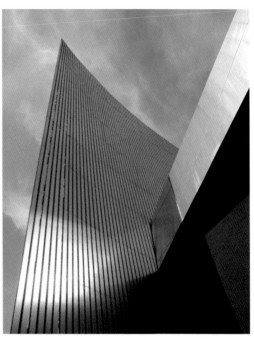

Imperial War Museum North.
Air shard from below

Imperial War Museum North. View from ship canal

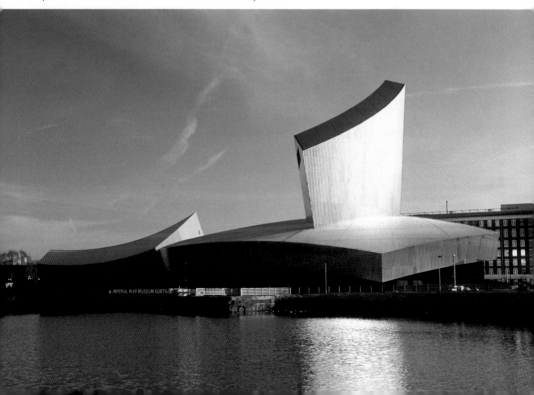

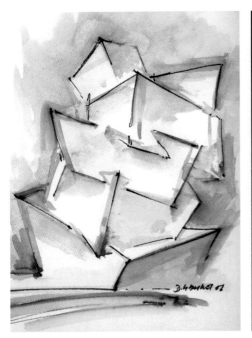

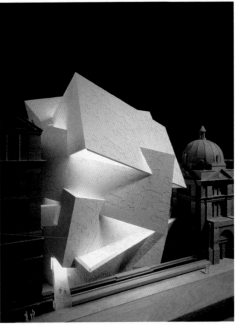

Victoria and Albert Museum, London.
The Spiral, watercolor

The Spiral.
Model, view from Exhibition Road

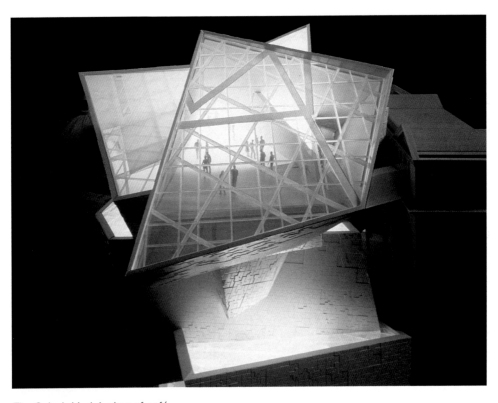

The Spiral. Model, view of café

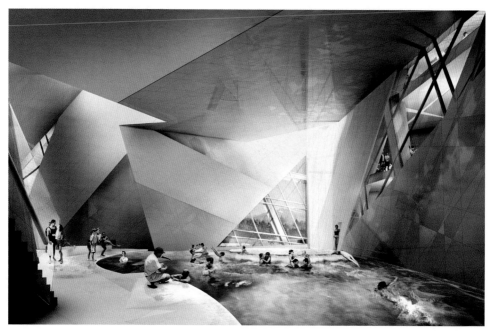

Westside, Brunnen, Switzerland. Rendering of swimming facility

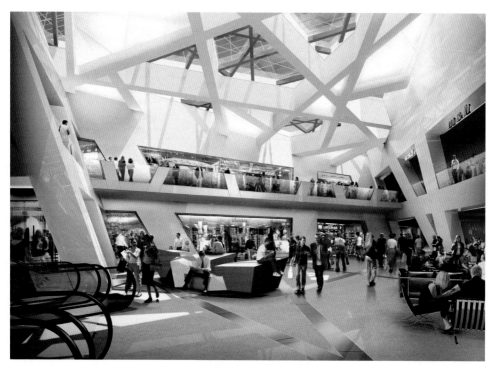

Westside. Rendering of mall

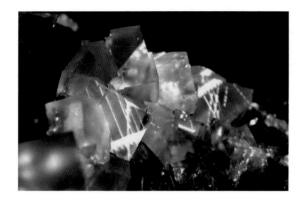

Study of light projection through crystal for Royal Ontario Museum, Toronto.

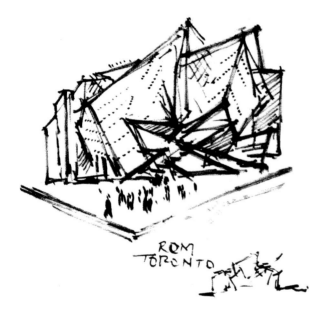

Royal Ontario Museum. Original competition sketch, on a napkin

Royal Ontario Museum. Northeast view rendering

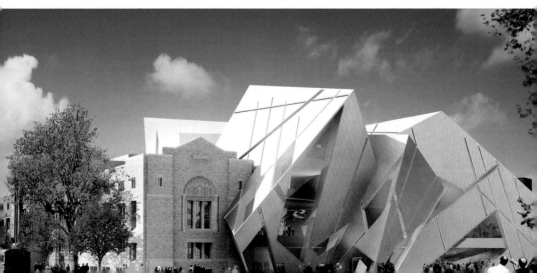

Royal Ontario
Museum.
Aerial rendering
of the Crystal and
historic buildings

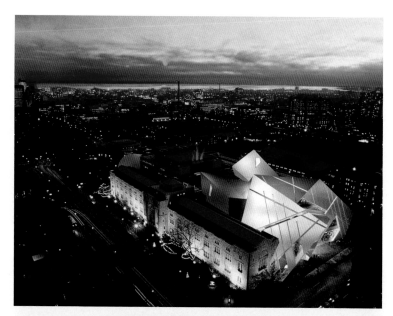

Royal Ontario
Museum.
Rendering
of interior of
Spirit House

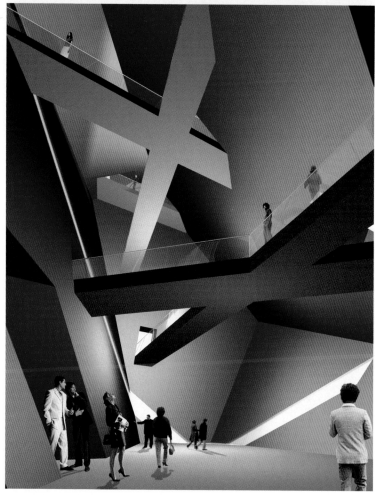

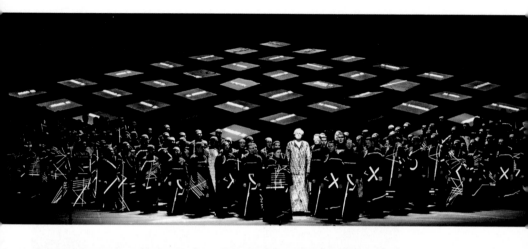

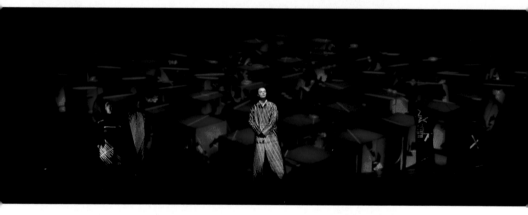

Stage set, lighting, and costume design for Olivier Messiaen's *Saint François d'Assise* at the Deutsche Oper Berlin

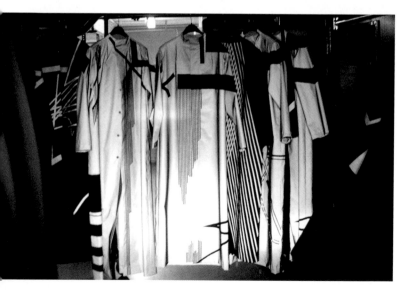

Costumes of the chorus for *Saint François d'Assise*

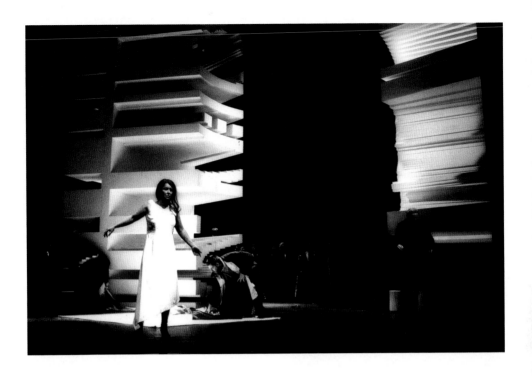

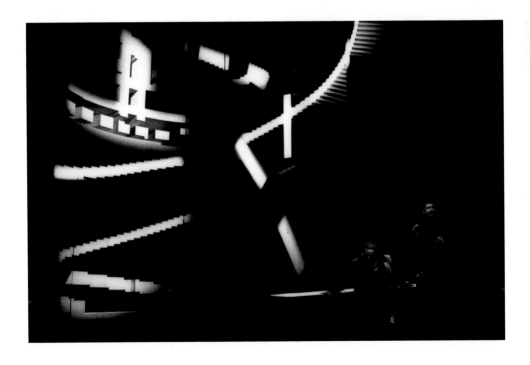

Stage set and costume design for Richard Wagner's *Tristan und Isolde* at the Saarbrücken Oper

Danish Jewish Museum,
Copenhagen.
Original watercolor
concept sketch

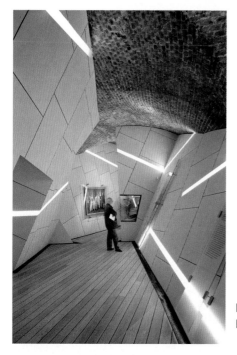

Danish Jewish Museum.
Exhibition space

Danish Jewish Museum. Main entrance

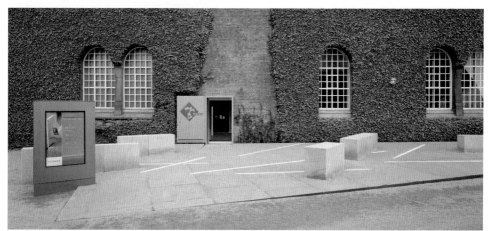

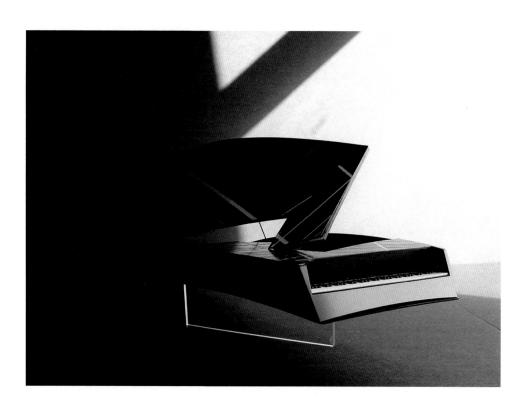

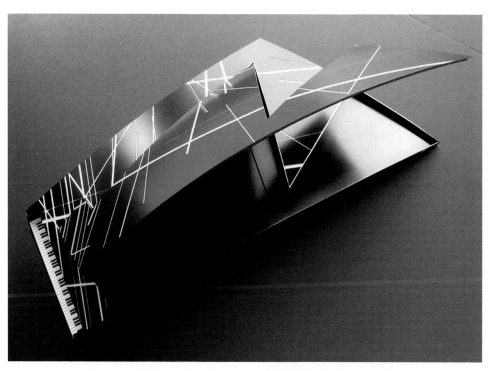

Schimmel grand piano. Model, two views

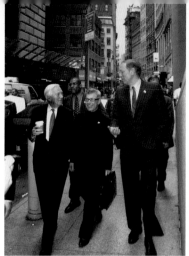

John Whitehead, me, and Governor
George Pataki, lower Manhattan

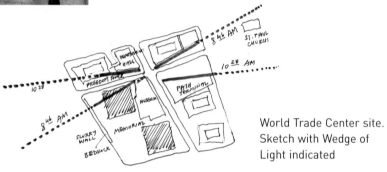

World Trade Center site.
Sketch with Wedge of
Light indicated

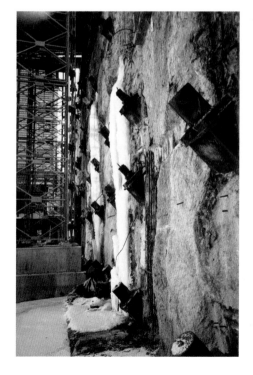

Slurry Wall at Liberty Street

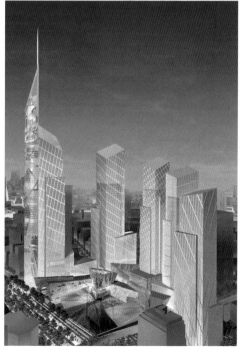

World Trade Center site. Rendering

World Trade Center site. Rendering of lower Manhattan PATH terminal

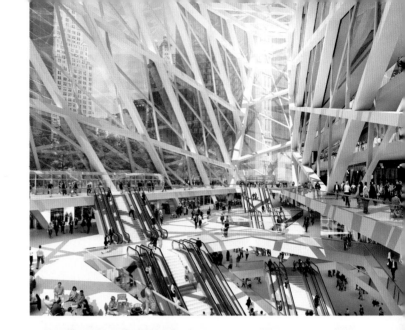

World Trade Center site. Rendering of September 11 Place, east view

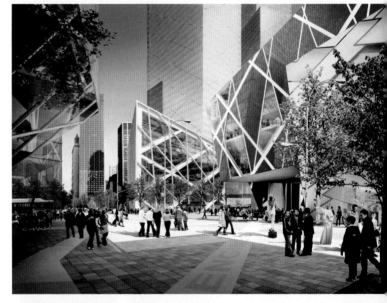

World Trade Center site. Rendering of performing arts center at Greenwich and Fulton streets

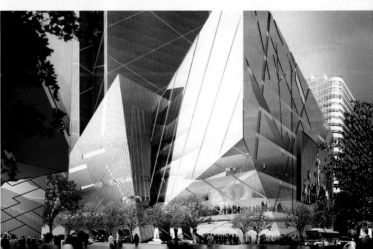

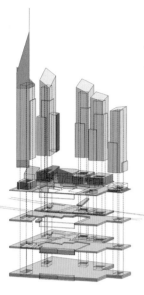

World Trade Center. Vertical distribution of uses with underground infrastructure

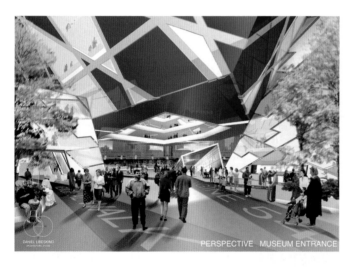

World Trade Center site. Rendering of museum entrance, with slurry wall visible in the background

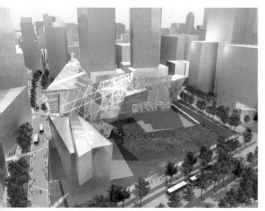

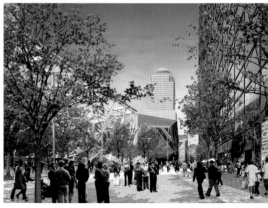

World Trade Center site. Rendering of proposed memorial and cultural buildings

World Trade Center site. Rendering of Wedge of Light, from the east

With Nina, celebrating the opening of the Jewish Museum building, Berlin, January 1999

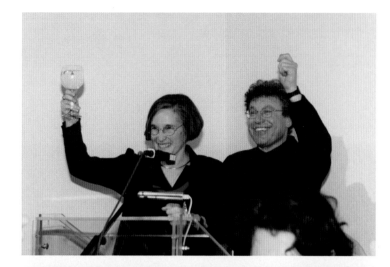

Lev, Rachel, and Noam at the opening of the Felix Nussbaum Museum, 1998

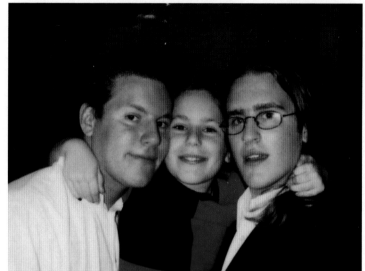

Returning to Poland in 2004, and the courtyard where I first lived

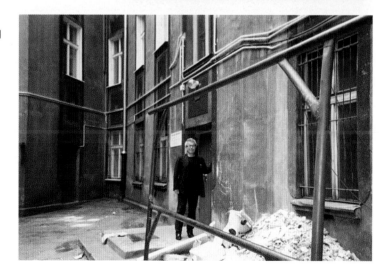

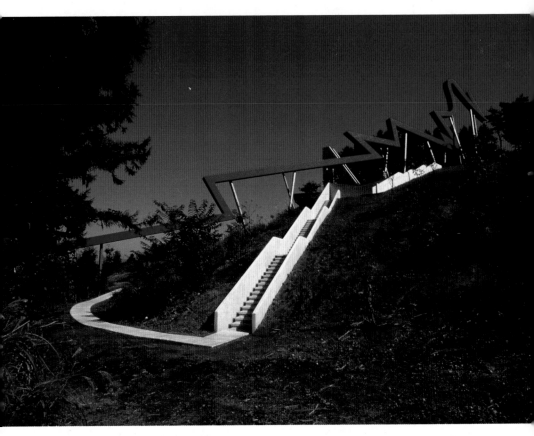

Symbol of the city of Uozu, built into a mountain overlooking the Sea of Japan

work, and decided to build a small museum to commemorate their native son. I entered the competition to design the building, and won. It was not the first architectural competition I'd won, but it was the first of the buildings I designed that was completed.

In designing the museum, I tried not to be sentimental about Nussbaum. I was determined to design something that would honor not the victims of the Holocaust in general, but the story of one individual and his fate. A man. A face. I wanted visitors to *see* Nussbaum.

The building consists of three intersecting parts. One is clad in wood, another in sheet metal, and one is simply exposed concrete. This last volume is less a building than a big tunnel, long and dark, with the two-story-high Nussbaum-gang, or Nussbaum Passage, inside. It is there that Nussbaum's last works have been hung, those he did just before the Gestapo took him away. In his journals he bemoaned the cramped quarters in which he was forced to work. He had no perspective, he complained; it was impossible to step back and capture a whole face. Still, he painted and drew in a kind of delirium, and it is these paintings and drawings, sometimes created only inches away from his face, that hang here— some set very high, others very low to the ground.

When the German regulators saw that the proposed passage was only about six feet wide, they tried to stop me. "You can't put such a narrow space in a public building," they objected. "This is a museum. People must be able to move freely." But this is what it was like, I told them. This is not about freedom of movement; this is about the compression of experience.

I called the project "Museum Without Exit," since there was no exit from the Holocaust for Felix Nussbaum.

On opening day, I watched as two lines of nuns, in full habit and perfect formation, crossed the bridge to enter the museum. Once you are inside, it's easy to lose your orientation; you follow labyrinthine corridors, and you come to dead ends. Often you are forced to retrace your steps. Lest it sound like work, I should add that people tend to find the experience uplifting and memorable.

I watched, fascinated, as the nuns moved about inside, trying to find their way. One came up to me, not knowing who I was. "I can't find out. Where is out? How do I get out of this building?" she demanded in German. There was panic in her voice.

"It's not a very large place," I said. "You'll find your way."

They all did, eventually. As they emerged, I could see they had been profoundly touched, even rattled, by what they had experienced. They had *seen* Nussbaum. And when they headed back over the bridge, they didn't reassemble into their ordered lines, but instead gathered in small groups, talking animatedly.

My architecture, which is often overtly expressive, unnerves some critics, many of whom perhaps are more comfortable in an antiseptic world where emotions can be kept at bay and buildings can be discussed in purely aesthetic terms.

Since the modernist era began, buildings have been designed to turn a neutral face to the world, to be immune to expression. The goal has been to produce objective, not subjective, architecture. But here is the truth of the matter: No building, no matter how neutral it is supposed to be, *is* actually neutral. Le Corbusier may have insisted that "a house is a machine for living in," but even if you live in the most perfectly minimalist, perfectly white loft, it is still an expression of your personality, and hence not a neutral space.

Mies van der Rohe's New National Gallery in Berlin is thought by some to be the most objective building ever built, the glass box to end all glass boxes—just a flat, black roof, eight columns, and a glass façade. No expression, right? Yet there's a violence in the radical way it strips all but the most essential elements away. Its nakedness assaults us, overwhelms. It makes us self-conscious. It is one of the more aggressive buildings I have seen.

Take another building: the expansion of the Museum of Modern Art in New York designed by Yoshio Taniguchi. What is being built as I write is an anonymous glass skyscraper. A "cool white box," says *The New York Times*, with admiration. "This is not destination architecture," the museum director boasts, as if it would be tacky to construct a building that excites people. But this cool box that is being built is making a surprisingly radical statement, because it is such an aggressive expression of corporate power. By selecting this design, the museum director and others have chosen to express the profile of MoMA—that MoMA is the dominant force in the world of corporate museums— and the building's apparent neutrality strengthens its statement about power and its formidable presence in the art world.

One of the most exciting buildings ever built is Louis Kahn's Kimbell Art Museum in Forth Worth. All buildings are difficult to describe, but this is one of the most challenging. I can tell you that it consists of sixteen vaulted units grouped into three sections consisting of parallel rows, and I can tell you that it's made of reinforced concrete, but that utterly fails to tell you what it looks and feels like. I urge you to look it up, because it's a magnificent design. Kahn's very formal architecture is created out of formal blocks, and by all rights the building should be cold and coldhearted. Instead there is a rare poetry to it. Kahn was an artist who did nothing by formula, and who loved what he was doing, and that love was expressed in his work. He once said something along the lines of: The world didn't know it needed Beethoven's Fifth Symphony until it heard it, and then once it was played, it was unimaginable to exist without it. The same could be said in architecture for the Kimbell.

Kahn's building opened in 1972. Thirty years later, the Modern Art Museum, an addition designed by the architect Tadao Ando, opened across the street. Using the Kimbell as his guide, Ando, an otherwise excellent architect, strove to create a modern-day reincarnation. Just as Kahn had done, he used concrete as his primary material, and he used it perfectly. That didn't matter in the end, though, because, disappointingly, his museum turned out to be an anonymous concrete box.

Who wants to be trapped in an anonymous box?

I was struggling to determine where the original concept of the neutral box came from, and then I had it: the Stoics. In the stretch of history when the pagan era was waning, and before Christianity swept the Western world, the Stoics developed a philosophy that must have seemed ideal for dealing with turbulent times: Walk through the world as if you were not a part of it. Master all passions, and be dispassionate, cool, indifferent to the outer world.

Undoubtedly, this lifestyle was effective for some. But indifference is not a virtue. And neutrality is not a value. A cool box building has no place in this world—the world is enriched not by neutrality or indifference, but by passions and beliefs.

In June 2004, another building of mine, the Danish Jewish Museum, opened in Copenhagen. It's small, and it tells the remarkable story of how most of Denmark's Jews were smuggled out of the country in the middle of the night, and taken on fishing boats to the safety of neutral Sweden. It's an unusual building, made of wood, like the boats, and like boats rocking over waves, it is undulating in shape.

"Mr. Libeskind, there are no right angles in your building," a Danish television interviewer commented.

"That's definitely true," I responded.

"But how can you have this?" he asked. Now, the Danes tend to be quite obsessed with boxes. They are Lutheran in religious tradition, puritanical in spirit. If cultures could be defined by angles, theirs would be a right-angle culture. "Not even the floor is a right angle in any way," the interviewer continued, beginning to sound agitated.

I did my best to calm him. "You know, you live in a democracy," I said. "There are three hundred fifty-nine other angles. Why would you insist on this single, solitary one?"

He burst out laughing.

It is true, you know: There are so many possibilities, and yet we often feel compelled to march to a single tune or beat. There's a presumption, and I think it began with the modernists, that right angles and repetition provide us with a necessary sense of order. It is what one is taught in architecture school. My first project at Cooper Union was what is called a "nine-square problem." You are given nine squares and told to design a building with them. I instantly rebelled. It would be like painting by numbers. And yet everyone in architecture starts this way—with a square and a grid on a piece of paper. The tyranny of the grid! I fight against it all the time: buildings designed like checkerboards, with repetitive units that march along the same track. A marching grid is not what life is about.

So prevalent is the idea of the grid that the architect Josef Kleihues actually hands his employees a piece of paper already divided into grids, in which every facet of the design— the placement of the toilet, the shape of the doors—has been marked, down to the millimeter. The grid imposes an unnecessarily restrictive pattern on experience. Misbegotten too, because the notion of the grid promises that it can impose order on chaos. Its clean right angles and geometric rigor feel scientific. But this is as outmoded a sense of science as is the study of physiognomy to determine human behavior. It makes me think of German architects of the 1920s who wore white coats, the kind laboratory technicians wear, as if they were involved in surgical operations.

The universe is now seen as even more fantastically ordered than we ever imagined. In physics, chemistry, cosmology, we see the universe in terms of string theory. In particle physics, one talks of waves, energies, chaos theory. No one expects a unified set of shapes. There is so much more complexity in the world than we tend to admit. Even those of us who live fairly quiet lives don't experience ourselves as monolithic. So why settle for buildings based on a regimented formula that denies human desire and is antithetical to the quality of life? What good is a putative sense of order, if it's a false sense of order?

In my travels, I have seen some incredible things, architecture that defies rigidity and precedent, that demonstrates the imaginative and emotional range of its creators. When I was a child I saw the salt mines of Wieliczka, near Kraków, which date back to the thirteenth century, with their enormous underground chambers, more than two thousand of them, filled with astonishing salt sculptures. There are whole cities carved down there, and underground salt lakes, totally transparent and yet magically black because they're deprived of light. There are salt chapels, large ones, ornamented with carvings of crucifixes and salt chandeliers. Goethe and Schiller wrote about them; Pope John Paul II has visited them. These are cities built not to be used, staircases constructed not to be climbed. This is not about form following function. This is about the true human spirit—the spirit that dreams and aspires to and achieves great things.

Similarly surreal, and just as fascinating, are the chapels found in Eastern Europe, Portugal, and Italy made of human bones, including skulls. The skulls are both the foundation *and* the decoration, and hundreds upon hundreds of them create a crazy-quilt pattern, from the altar to the ceiling and out to the doors. When I tell people about these chapels, they imagine the killing fields of Cambodia, where skulls were displayed in a sickening show of evil triumphant. But many of these chapels were built during the Black Death as a form of redemption, and to celebrate the resurrection of souls that the builders believed had moved on to a better place.

There's a wall I love, a clay-tiled wall along the rock garden at Ryoanji, a Zen temple in northwestern Kyoto. The garden is one of the wonders of the world. Out of a surface of raked white sand emerge fifteen stones; yet no matter where you stand, you can see only fourteen. They say that if you find the right spot, you can take them all in, but I've yet to manage that. They also tell you that contemplating the garden can be spiritually transporting. That I *have* managed, although it takes time, and the waiting can be hard. You need to keep an open mind and an open heart, and then something sweeps over you. Exactly what that is cannot easily be put into words, but it is personal and profound.

The wall I love at Ryoanji is made of tiles with striking imperfections in which you can see the transformation of time. In Japan, there's a technique of pottery noted for its imperfections, called *raku*. As with the flaws purposefully introduced into patterns by Persian carpet weavers, the notion is that perfection itself is a sterile thing and that true perfection incorporates human imperfection.

When I'm working on a building, I often find myself poring over photographs of faces. When I designed the Jewish Museum in Berlin, for example, I sat for hours looking at images of people walking around Alexanderplatz in the 1930s. I stared at the faces of the twelve-tone composer Arnold Schoenberg and his friend the abstract painter Wassily Kandinsky; I committed to memory the piercing gaze of the literary critic Walter Benjamin. You won't see a direct link between the photos and the building that eventually went up. I didn't imagine these men walking into it. But when I looked into their faces, I could feel something personal and primal and very human, which I tried to incorporate into my design.

The builders of the Baroque period firmly believed that stones have to tell the story of time, of history, of mortality. I love that about the period, and I love too the essential philosophy behind the movement. The word *baroque* is related to the Italian *barocco*, meaning "bizarre," but in fact it is closer to "full of life," "exuberant." *Barocco* refers also to a pearl that is wonderfully and naturally flawed, and therefore beautiful but unlike any other. Like a person. Like a face.

Once when people wrote about Mozart, they often brought up one physical characteristic: his nose. Mozart was a little man—some said dwarfish—and his nose was huge, pointy, and hooked. He even composed a piece of music that required two hands and a nose in order to hit all the notes. But of course even more remarkable than the protuberance was the very specific, haunting quality of his music. As the conductor Georg Solti once said, "Mozart makes you believe in God." What is it about Mozart's music that makes it so distinctive? Even someone new to music can tell, from the opening bars, that a work is Mozart's, and not a piece by Salieri or another composer of the day, although Mozart was definitely of his time. "What is your secret?" he was asked. He replied: "It's the shape of my nose, the music is in the shape of my nose." It's a classic Mozart answer—silly, almost childish in one regard, brilliant in another. The music is singularly personal and individual. It is divine, but at the same time it is very human.

In Denver, I was shown a beautiful mock-up of a piece of the museum expansion, measuring roughly ten feet across. Before you build a building, you create mock-ups so there will be as few surprises as possible when you go to work on the real thing. We were studying the titanium in which the building will be clad. There is a mystery in titanium—it is indestructible, lightweight but extremely resilient. Bicycles are made from it, and so are airplanes. Denver is a titanium town, home to the world's largest supplier, so it made great sense to use it as cladding. But it is prohibitively expensive—unless you are lucky enough to be Frank Gehry building the Guggenheim in Bilbao, or unless you are as lucky as we have been, because on hearing that we couldn't afford to purchase it, Lanny Martin, head of Timet (Titanium Metals Corporation), headquartered in Denver, generously said the company would donate what was needed.

I love titanium's luminosity. Because of its density, titanium is very subtly reflective, unlike steel and aluminum, which are more obvious, more pleasing to those who like shiny buildings. Titanium is also very tactile, which makes some people uncomfortable; when you touch it, your fingerprints leave impressions on the surface. I like to see the tainted surfaces, as they suggest visitors' engagement with the building.

We were looking at the mock-up, admiring it intensely, when, abruptly, disappointment hit me. The construction workers who were gathered around could sense it. "What's wrong?" someone asked.

"It's perfect," I replied.

"I know," one man said, running his finger over the stunningly smooth surface, and admiring the seamless way in which the sheets of metal hooked up.

"No," I said. "I don't think you do. It's too perfect."

I don't ask human beings to behave like machines; I don't want them to. I like human beings to behave like human beings, and I'm ready to tolerate things that are slightly off. The workers couldn't believe it, and my associate architects grappled to understand my problem too. "So, you don't want perfect."

"I do want perfect," I said. "I just want it with human imperfections."

One of the men smiled. "That shouldn't be too hard," he said.

·6

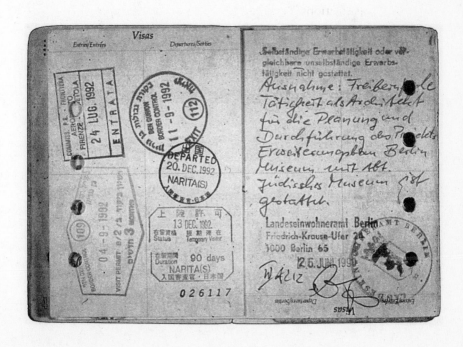

For a brief moment at the end of the 1980s when the Wall fell, it appeared that the united Berlin might be poised to become, architecturally, a first-tier city—a city of the twenty-first century, a city to take on Tokyo or Paris or London. The economy was booming, and some of the world's most well-known architects—Philip Johnson, Jean Nouvel, Henry Cobb—were preparing to build bold, new buildings in the former (and future) German capital. My good friend from Milan the architect and philosopher Aldo Rossi had been awarded the commission for what promised to be his crowning achievement, a new national museum, to be built opposite the Reichstag. Steven Holl was about to receive the commission for the American Memorial Library. And we were to begin work on the Jewish Museum.

And then came Herr Stimmann.

Every city has powerful building officials. But Berlin is, and always has been, different: its building director commands a greater power than most, far greater than that of the senator of building. He is a veritable czar. And yet, in 1992, when Hans Stimmann was appointed, we had no idea who he was; but we felt the poisonous impact of his presence, and limited vision, immediately. Although he was a focused, energetic, and masterful manager, his appointment was disastrous both for Berlin and for architecture.

Right after he was appointed, Stimmann summoned me to his office to present the museum project once again (once again!). When I finished my presentation, he turned to the people in the room—his administrative aides and members of my staff. "This building is an architectural fart," he said. "And if I had been here one year ago, it never would have gone ahead. But I guess it will, Mr. Libeskind." Then he continued to rant: "I'm sick and tired of all this Jewish history. We've got too much Jewish history in Berlin as it is. We don't need any more." The room was stunned into embarrassed silence. I got up and left in disgust.

Stimmann's antagonism toward me and my architecture was relentless. He hated my kind of architecture, and his feelings about me weren't much helped by the fact that I had become known around Berlin as a "Jewish architect" and was frequently called on to speak about Jewish culture and history—the very stuff of which Stimmann was sick and tired. I hated being pigeonholed as a "Jewish architect," but not as much as being hated by Stimmann.

It was soon evident that Stimmann was determined to keep us from building anything in Berlin, even a phone booth. We'd won commissions for many projects in the city. Stimmann intervened, and blocked them all.

We did have one real ally in the government: Ulrich Stangel. A soft-spoken, older man, Stangel wasn't very high up in
the bureaucracy, but he knew how to guide us through its
knotty corridors of power. He alone in the government
seemed to grasp how important a building like the Jewish Museum could be for all Berliners. "Your building is going to have
as much impact on Berlin as Mies van der Rohe's National
Gallery, and Scharoun's music hall," he would tell me insis-
tently, ardently. To build it, he would say, Germans will need
Herzblut—heart's blood. And, he would add, they will get it.

When we moved to Berlin in 1989, most members of our extended family were horrified. They declared they would never
visit us, never set foot in the city in which the Holocaust was
devised. But my father was not one to ignore history, and
when he visited that fall, he wanted to see everything. I took
him to Potsdamer Platz, in its glory days the commercial center of Berlin, and home to the first European traffic light.
Now it was a no-man's-land, cut in two by the Berlin Wall.
As we walked along the so-called Death Strip, where East
Germans who jumped their side of the Wall were shot, my father suddenly stopped. "Look at me," he said. "Here I am.
Hitler is nothing but ashes. But I am here, and I am living,
eating, sleeping in this city, and below, Hitler's bones are rot-
ting!" His eyes glistened with tears but he sounded victorious.

When, soon after that, thousands poured into the streets

to bring the Wall down with their own hands, I felt an ambivalence. Of course I was heartened that the same totalitarian system that had oppressed my family was in its death throes. But the huge crowds of Germans wandering the streets brought back terrifying associations from the past. And I had to wonder: How would German history be regarded in this new era of unification? Would there be a further forgetting, a greater distancing? Would history become an abstraction?

The rebuilding of Potsdamer Platz began shortly after the Wall came down. It had all the markings of a grand project. Many of the most famous names in architecture were invited to build there: Richard Rogers, Arata Isozaki, Renzo Piano, Rafael Moneo, all of whom are capable of designing wonderful buildings. What was actually built, though, was not their best work, not by a long shot. Berlin's Building Administration wanted the names of the great architects but not their visions.

Some master plans and their directives free architects to go beyond themselves, to be as creative as they can be. Others . . . well, others don't. None of the designs offered for Potsdamer Platz addressed Berlin's complicated history; none managed to touch the city's deeper spirit, both good and bad. When I walk through the area's streets now, I often feel as if I were walking through a computer simulation, a virtual reality as thin and flat and ultimately as lifeless as a computer screen.

Despite Stimmann's invective, I was invited to join a

competition in 1993 to design the master plan for Alexander-platz, which is roughly two miles northeast of Potsdamer Platz. Like Potsdamer Platz, it had been razed during World War II, but afterward the East German government had turned it into a highly developed commercial center with Soviet-imposed buildings both grandiose and kitsch. The Stalinallee, the main avenue from the East into Alexander-platz, was the pride of the communist system. The veneer of the monstrously monolithic apartment complexes hid the de-caying prefabricated blocks from which they were con-structed. Their enormous scale and style were intended to overwhelm the individual. What struck me most intensely when I visited was the resounding emptiness. Before the war, the square had vibrated with life and with potential. Now it was a virtual tomb.

For me, Alexanderplatz had a special meaning. As a boy in Lodz, I viewed it as the epitome of the sophistication of communist Europe. German postage stamps featured images of the tall department stores that rose above the square, and I remember peering at the stamps and longing to visit the city. To me it represented a world of material goods that were unavailable in dreary Lodz.

I was excited by the challenge of restoring vitality to Alexanderplatz and finding a way for the area to be both an embodiment of the city's past and a lifeline to its future. But as I studied the Planning Department's directives and the technical requirements, I decided on a strategy to preserve the existing buildings even though they were certainly not beautiful. I was not about to follow the organizer's goal of erasing the history of the site, an explicit exercise in amnesia. A city is not a tabula rasa or a plaything for an architect's imagination. So I re-created the context by designing streets with a human scale and by proposing a dramatic architecture freed, at last, from totalitarian conformity. I was inspired to do so when I read Alfred Döblin's 1929 novel *Berlin Alexanderplatz*. As well as a writer, Döblin had been a doctor committed to the poorer workers in and around Alexanderplatz. I used his left palm print, which I took from an illustration in his book, and the lifelines on that palm, to organize the area and the orientation of the buildings.

More than two thousand people came to Berolina-Haus in the fall of 1993 to see the architectural presentations. It was an unforgettable sight. East Berliners lined the walls of a packed auditorium, listening intently as each of the five finalists explained their designs in the allotted fifteen minutes. This was the people's first taste of democracy. Two architects were booed off the stage. My scheme connected with the audience and became the favorite of the East Berliners. But Herr Stimmann wouldn't have it. One of the architects whom the audience had jeered got the job, but his plan lacked the very thing that Herr Stangel recognized Berliners were so desperate for: *Herzblut*. The public's voice was never on the agenda. Berlin is not New York.

I was alone in my Berlin office on a Saturday evening, working on some drawings, when the doorbell rang. There stood Philip Johnson. He was dressed in an immaculate suit and a fedora, his familiar round black-framed glasses adding, as always, a definitive touch.

"I came to see this museum of yours," he said. "Berlin is my favorite city, so I want to see what you're doing to it."

I first got to know Philip Johnson, the godfather of American architecture, in 1988. He was creating a widely discussed and controversial exhibition on what he termed "Deconstructivist" architecture at the Museum of Modern Art in New York. It was the first time in decades that an architecture exhibit had been shown in the main gallery on the ground floor, and it was a big deal—and an enormous opportunity for me to be included, because I was relatively unknown at the time. It was an honor to be considered alongside such architects as Frank Gehry, Peter Eisenman, Zaha Hadid, Bernard Tschumi, Rem Koolhaas, and the members of Coop Himmelb(l)au.

I went to visit Johnson in his Manhattan penthouse apartment, which overlooked his AT&T building, with its postmodern Chippendale pediment. Staring straight at the skyscraper, which had become the leading symbol of postmodernism, Johnson said, "You know, those architects are going to be surprised tomorrow when they wake up and find this whole style, this whole postmodernist business, gone—including my own building right here." He gestured at the AT&T and laughed—laughed at his own work!

Now in Berlin to deliver a lecture, Johnson was feeling nostalgic. He had been an international wunderkind. In 1932, as director of MoMA's department of architecture, he had established modernism's preeminence with a seminal show on the International Style. Le Corbusier, Mies van der Rohe, Gropius—he had introduced them all to the provincial audiences of the United States. Not yet twenty-six, he was charismatic, openly gay, and he'd obviously had a hell of a good time in the heady, sophisticated Berlin of that era.

"Let's see this building of yours," he said, and I took him on a tour of the models and drawings scattered around the office.

"My God," he exclaimed, "it's not possible that this building is actually going to get built, is it?"

"I think it will," I replied, ever the optimist.

"*Ich wache endlich auf . . .*" he recited. "I finally wake up."

Alas, in the following years, Johnson's battle-scarred skepticism was to prove more accurate than my optimism. The challenges rarely let up, and there were constant obstacles to overcome.

Of all the challenges to the Jewish Museum, the gravest came in the summer of 1991, on July 3. Nina was at an ATM on the Ku'damm the next day, when she felt a tap on her back.

It was Michael Cullen, an American writer living in Berlin. "I'm so sorry about what happened last night," he said.

Nina had no idea what he was talking about.

"You didn't see the news this morning? The Senate canceled the museum yesterday. It was scrapped by unanimous vote."

We had heard vague rumors in recent weeks, but had no idea we were in such danger. We hadn't even known there was a vote pending.

We couldn't fight the unanimous vote of the Berlin Senate. But Nina wasn't ready to pack it in; she started working the phones. *What happened?* she wanted to know.

Well, there had been a few changes, she was told. One: The Senate had decided to support a serious bid for Berlin to host a future Olympics, and to do so, senators felt they needed to appropriate the equivalent of $50 million previously earmarked for the museum. Two: Even without the possibility of the Olympics, unification was proving far more expensive than anyone had dreamed. And finally, it seemed possible that they were now thinking there really wasn't a need for a Jewish Museum, after all.

It had been our bleakest day. The boys were out on the town, and Rachel, an active two-year-old now, was down for the night. Nina poured me a glass of wine, and we sat in silence. Then she put her glass down. "Libeskind," she said, "I think we can save this building."

"But how can we?" I asked despairingly. "We have no power here."

Nina was strangely calm. "You have to promise to stay out of it completely."

Stay out of it? How could I stay out of it?

"The fight will make you insane. It's best if you concentrate on the architecture, and leave the politics to me."

My wife comes from a remarkable family. You do not want to inflame a Lewis. Her father, David Lewis, was a poor Russian Jew who landed in Canada in his early teens, went on to be a Rhodes Scholar at Oxford, and returned to Canada to become one of its great progressive leaders. He founded and headed the New Democratic Party, and was a member of Parliament until the 1970s. Nina's brother Stephen was a leader of the NDP in Ontario and a member of the provincial legislature before being named Canadian ambassador to the United Nations. He is now the UN secretary-general's special envoy for HIV/AIDS in Africa. Her brother Michael and her twin sister, Janet, are also devoted to politics. Nina herself has managed political campaigns; progressive politics is in her blood.

She began the campaign by alerting the international press. News of the project's cancellation made papers around the world, and the coverage incited a full two months of debate in the national German and local Berlin media. Every time I picked up a paper or turned on the news, day or night, the museum and its fate were under discussion.

What would it mean to cancel it? Should Berlin spend money on it—or save the money for something else? East and

West Berlin both had been rich with cultural institutions. Now, after unification, the city found itself with no fewer than three opera houses and eight orchestras, scores of museums, and countless theaters. The German government and the Berlin Senate were reeling from the new financial responsibilities.

I went to sleep every night with deep anxiety. Could we—and our supporters—persuade officials to change their minds? In addition to thinking about bricks and mortar, I felt responsible to the millions who had died and to the new generation who shouldn't forget. As I saw Nina on the phone, her inscrutable expression supplying no indication as to whether things were going well or not, I felt we were one person sharing the discomfort and pain of uncertainty.

I spent days in a haze, drawing plans and elevations of the museum, which seemed to me like phantoms looking for life. I understood that all the best intentions in the world have no ultimate force against decisions beyond our control. It's always said that you can't fight city hall. But Nina did.

And she didn't let up. She organized a letter-writing campaign among influential political and cultural figures, including Benjamin Netanyahu, deputy foreign minister of Israel; Jerusalem mayor Teddy Kollek; the French minister of culture, Jacques Lang; and Rabbi Marvin Hier, the director of the Simon Wiesenthal Center in Los Angeles. A key supporter was Willy Brandt, a former mayor of West Berlin and chancellor of Germany, who had known Nina's

father in the 1960s. Now head of the German Social Democratic Party, Brandt lobbied a successor as chancellor, Hel-
mut Kohl. We depended as well on the support of respected
members of the Berlin cultural scene and local politicians,
such as Kristin Feireiss, Bernard Schneider, Thomas Gaeht-
gens, and Peter Raue.

There are many buildings that should be built but aren't.
Yet this was about more than a building; it was about the
meaning of the building, and the role it could play in moving all of Germany, not just Berliners, into a new century.
Here at last was a place where Germans might face their
history.

Some of our opponents surprised me. The ambivalence
within the Jewish community was tangible. Many Jews were
still terrified that if they became too visible, anti-Semitism
would rise again. And they had reason to feel vulnerable:
there were only some three thousand Jews living in Berlin
in the early 1990s. The leader of the community was a Polish Holocaust survivor named Heinz Galinski. He and other
survivors knew all too well that the last Jewish museum in
Berlin had opened in November 1933. It was closed immediately after. Galinski's reluctance to support our building melted, though, when we showed him the stack of
letters from around the world. His eyes widened as he read,
and then he extended his hand. "*Mazel tov.* You have my
support."

In the end, the pressure got to Berlin mayor Eberhard

Diepgen, who decided that he had no option but to step in. In September 1991, the senators relented and offered us about $150,000 to continue working until they made up their minds.

Great! I thought. This is great!

Nina knew better. "This is hush money," she told the mayor's aide, who nearly spilled coffee all over himself. "You are not going to bribe us with that. We are going to make this happen *now*."

The mayor tried a new tactic, and called us into his office in Schöneberg. President Kennedy had delivered his famous *"Ich bin ein Berliner"* speech in the nearby square, and as I entered the main hall, those words echoed in my mind. "I am not building this building as a foreigner," I told myself. "I'm not here as a tourist, and the mayor and I will fight this out, Berliner to Berliner."

"Herr Libeskind," Mayor Diepgen said, with patronizing formality, "I have an extraordinary proposition for you. As you know, we are most sorry that we cannot support your building. . . . It will be impossible to reverse the Senate's decision. . . . I would like to offer you instead, in the future, sky- scrapers in the new Alexanderplatz. Building skyscrapers here will not only make you very famous, it will make you very rich. Because you know what a museum is? It's nothing. It's a public project. But a commercial building means money and connections and fame."

Skyscrapers do indeed mean money and prestige.

I stood up. "Mayor Diepgen," I said, "I did not come to Berlin to build a skyscraper. I came to build the Jewish Museum, and that's what I am going to do."

The mayor broke into a cold sweat. Wet beads appeared across his brow. He had not imagined that I might turn down his offer. "But . . . but . . . I am giving you the chance to shape the future of the center of Berlin!" he said.

I had nothing more to say. I was not going to sell the museum out, for any building in the world.

The mayor's aide hurried after us as we left the building. "Didn't you get it?" he said. "The mayor just offered you a skyscraper on Alex! He'll put out a press release tomorrow!"

But I had made up my mind. If the Jewish Museum was scrapped, I would leave Berlin.

What we didn't know was that this would be Diepgen's last shot at trying to derail us. Like any politician, he was keenly attuned to the political consequences of his decisions. Later that day, a BBC television reporter stuck a microphone in his face. "Mr. Mayor, what is your decision?" he asked. "The whole world is watching." Diepgen tried to wave the reporter away but didn't succeed. "I've had it," he told his aide. "Do whatever it takes—but get that Libeskind woman off my back." His comment was recorded on the reporter's tape and broadcast on British television.

In October, the Parliament of Berlin unanimously overruled the Senate and voted to build the Jewish Museum. We were back on track.

Bit by bit, the museum took shape. One day I overheard a conversation between two kids who had wandered from the elementary school on the other side of Lindenstrasse.

"It's not a building," said the boy with certainty.

"Of course it is," the girl replied. "Look at all this equipment—this tractor, this bulldozer. It has to be a building."

"Doesn't look like any building I've ever seen," said the boy, still doubtful.

Sometimes it seemed that the only people who really appreciated the significance of the building were the construction workers and site engineers, who remained committed to it over its twisted and erratically funded twelve-year history. Then there were the hundreds of young people who sneaked into the construction site at night and later wrote to me about it.

One day, as I strolled through the site, the head glass-cutter came over and threw his arms around me. Roughly a thousand panes of glass would be used in the museum, each—with the exception of only five or so—unique in shape and cut. This man had made every one of them, and it had taken him about a year. "You've ruined my life!" he said with a big laugh. "This is the best job I've ever done, and I've now reached the limits of my profession. I'll never be able to go back to making normal windows!" I laughed too, and begged his forgiveness.

It was exhilarating, but the rest of my architectural practice in Berlin was frustrated. Though the museum was proceeding, I was worn out from the constant struggles. I
remember the day in 1994 when I turned to Nina and said,
"We've done our job with the museum. Let's leave Berlin."

Shortly thereafter I was offered a teaching position in Los
Angeles, at UCLA. Once again we looked forward to a new
start in California. We bade our Berlin friends farewell, and
packed our library. We renovated an office near the beach in
Santa Monica, sent the kids to school, and settled into our
new life.

We lived there for less than a year.

Suddenly, we won three competitions—all in Germany:
the Felix Nussbaum Museum in Osnabrück, the Philharmonic Hall in Bremen, and the Landsberger Allee land development project in eastern Berlin. Every week or two, I
traveled between California and Germany, a serious fifteen-
hour commute. I recall standing bleary-eyed in the Reykjavik
airport with Nina when she said, "Libeskind, it's time to move
back to Berlin."

We returned to find much confusion at the Jewish Museum.
What, precisely, was its mandate? What should its collection
be? Every time the Berlin government changed, and it
changed frequently, the museum's sense of mission shifted as
well. Even its name kept changing.

The museum's original director, and true friend, Dr. Rolf Bothe, suffered a heart attack and took a quieter post in the Baroque calm of the city of Weimar. An Israeli, Amnon Barzel, succeeded him, but it was soon evident that he intended to turn the museum into a contemporary art gallery, which made little sense to the Germans. Next came Tom Freudenheim, a professional curator from the United States. He had more experience than Barzel, but he seemed stymied by the German bureaucracy. Then, in 1998, W. Michael Blumenthal became president and CEO of the museum. Born in Berlin, Blumenthal had fled the Nazis by boat, lived in Shanghai under the Japanese occupation, and eventually made his way to the United States. The secretary of the treasury under Jimmy Carter, he offered powerful leadership and direction. He changed the name of the museum to the Jewish Museum, Berlin, thereby defining the institution's scope and mission.

In 1999, the Jewish Museum, Berlin, opened, empty. The empty museum was a perfect venue for a celebration, attended by the highest-ranking German elected officials, including Chancellor Gerhard Schroeder. After dinner, Schroeder went to the table where my father sat and, so that the ninety-year-old Nachman would not have to get up, knelt before him, held his hand, and said, "Mr. Libeskind, you must be so proud. Thank you for being here." What a moment for Nachman— and for me! Never in my Polish boyhood could I have imagined a day when the chancellor of Germany, the son of a Wehrmacht soldier killed in action during World War II, would kneel before my father and thank him for coming to Germany.

The fact that the building was empty when it opened seemed to be of no consequence to Berliners, thousands of whom lined up to tour it. For a decade, they had debated the museum's purpose; now they wanted to be let inside. During the first year, there were 350,000 visitors. Workers were still putting on finishing touches as the crowds poured in.

One day, two elderly Jewish women, Berlin-born Holocaust survivors now living in England, visited the museum. This was their first trip to Berlin since the war. They were on special assignment from London's *Evening Standard* newspaper. I accompanied them as, slowly, they approached the Holocaust Tower. After we entered, a heavy metal door swung shut with an unforgiving thud. It was winter, and the tower was unheated. From outside the tower you could hear children playing in the schoolyard across the street, trucks grinding past on Lindenstrasse, people talking on the museum grounds. Like Jewish Berliners during the war, we were all cut off from normal daily life. The two elderly women broke into tears.

Berliners understood the building, deep in their hearts. They stood in the Holocaust Tower, silently, many with tears in their eyes. They studied the staircase, and knew why it dead-ended at a blank white wall. They walked through the garden in groups, talking quietly. The building resonated with the people of Berlin, and made me feel that working on a single building for twelve years was worth it.

From January 1999 to September 2001, Michael Blumenthal and his staff filled the museum with items for exhibition. In a very short time, the exhibition design firm and curators obtained everything they could from two thousand years of German Jewish history. The museum hosted an international gala to celebrate the museum's first exhibitions—it was no longer an empty building. The Chicago Philharmonic under Daniel Barenboim played Mahler's Seventh Symphony in Hans Scharoun's concert hall. After the concert, people made their way, through a rainy night, to the museum. The streets were closed off, and sharpshooters stood on nearby buildings.

The dinner party was held in the Baroque Berlin Museum. Once again the chancellor, the president, all the federal ministers of government, all the premiers of the provinces, all the leaders of the major Jewish organizations, members of the international Jewish community, city officials, and other dignitaries, including Henry Kissinger and Bill Bradley, were there. Newspaper headlines reported that on that evening, Berlin had come of age.

Blumenthal announced that the museum was now designated a federal one, thus elevating it from local to national institution. Under Blumenthal's leadership, the museum saw a final name change: now it would be called the Jewish Museum Berlin: Two Millennia of German Jewish History.

It had survived five name changes, four changes of government, three changes of director, and the turmoil of the last years of the twentieth century in Europe. At last the Jewish Museum Berlin was open. I went home that night with the burden of completing it off my shoulders for the first time in a dozen years. It was Saturday, September 8, 2001.

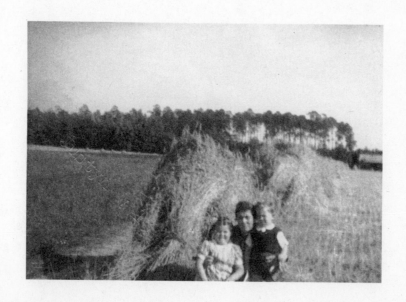

7

When he heard that I had joined the competition to design a World Trade Center master plan, a friend in Denver laughed a knowing laugh. "Daniel, you're going to be working for a lot of pharaohs," he cautioned. "Like eight million of them." He was right. We were going to have to listen to all of New York. And I was ready.

In the weeks leading up to the December 18, 2002, Winter Garden presentations, all the finalists had worked on their proposals in secrecy. Now our ideas were before the public, and *everyone* had an opinion. New Yorkers dove into the debate as only New Yorkers can. When I'd walk down the street, doormen would call out to me. Strangers cornered me to argue the finer points of my scheme or to open their hearts to me. Upon returning from a quick trip to Berlin, I was detained by a customs inspector at JFK. "I know you," he said. "So which one are you?" As I tried to figure out his question, he helped me: "I mean, are you the kissing one, the tic-tac-toe one, skeletons, or the one with the circle?" He drew a loop in the air with his index finger.

Ah. The kissing one was the Norman Foster design; tic-tac-toe was Meier–Eisenman–Gwathmey–Holl; skeletons was THINK; and yes, we were the circle. I loved it: This guy had grasped the most radical aspect of my plan, one that had been overlooked by almost everybody else. In the city famous for its grid, I wanted to build a huge circle. I wanted to surround and shelter the Ground Zero memorial with a ring of embracing towers.

"The circle, yes, that's mine," I said.

"Good," he told me, "that's the one I like," and he waved me through.

There were days when I was made to feel like a rock star. *The New York Times* interviewed me about my cowboy boots (which, frankly, are excellent); soon after, a reporter quizzed me on my glasses. I tried to impress him with the utilitarian aspects of the style (they don't fog up), but he was more interested in who the designer was. *Rolling Stone* asked me to contribute a list of items for its "Cool" issue. I suggested fusion, Emily Dickinson, the Bible, and the Bronx.

When the attention became overwhelming, as it soon did, Nina took to walking a few steps behind me. It made her look like a pasha's bride, but it also afforded her a measure of privacy.

From mid-December until early February, some 80,000 visitors swarmed the Winter Garden lobby to get a look at the architectural models. They lined up before the doors opened at seven a.m.; they had to be shooed home by the guards when the doors closed at eleven p.m. The place was always mobbed. Ten thousand comments were received. A website set up by the Lower Manhattan Development Corporation counted eight million hits. We were deluged with letters and e-mails; Nina sought to answer every one.

There were LMDC meetings, and Port Authority meetings, and community meetings, and meetings with representatives from the Metropolitan Transportation Authority and the New York State Department of Transportation, and presentations to Larry Silverstein. And there were meetings with the Families. Since 9/11, a number of groups had been formed by family members of the victims. To introduce us to their many concerns, LMDC board member Christy Ferrer—whose husband, Neil Levin, the head of the Port Authority, had died in the attacks—invited us to meet with representatives from at least ten groups. They told us about family members and friends they had lost, and where they suspected their loved ones had been when the planes hit.

The accounts were heart-wrenching. We met Tom Rogér, who remains a friend. His daughter, a flight attendant, was not supposed to be on American Airlines Flight 11, which crashed into the North Tower, but at the last moment she had agreed to cover for a colleague. Her parents did not know she was on the plane and, for that day and night, had no idea where she was. We met the mother of a young woman whose office had moved from midtown to a high floor in one of the towers at the beginning of 2001. Phobic about heights, the woman resisted going to work; she took a leave of absence and sought psychiatric help. After several months, feeling that she had sufficiently mastered her fear, she returned to work— on September 6. Five days later she was dead. A rabbi told us about a congregant who worked in one of the towers and was friends with a heavyset, wheelchair-bound colleague. After the plane hit the tower, office workers were urged to rush down the stairs, but the congregant refused to leave his friend, who was too heavy to be carried down the stairs. He stayed with his friend, and died. For me one of the most affecting moments came when a son spoke about his father, who had died earlier, in the 1993 World Trade Center bombing. A decade had passed, and the son was more composed than the others, but his anger was deeper, perhaps because he knew that so many of the security questions raised in the aftermath of the bombing had never been properly addressed. He felt that the people who died in the towers this time needn't have perished.

"Promise me you'll pay attention to what has to be done," he demanded.

We gave him our word.

We listened to many terrible tales, and we cried and took

notes. We wanted to make sure that something right could come out of this horrible wrong.

It filtered back to us that some of our competitors were mocking the earnestness of our approach. The American-flag pin in my lapel struck them as cornball. They'd roll their eyes when I mentioned the Declaration of Independence. "Oh my God," Rafael Viñoly said dismissively to a member of the Families whose support he was seeking. "Libeskind and his slurry wall. He's turning the whole thing into his own personal Wailing Wall."

In spite of my penchant for wearing black, I *am* more cornball than cosmopolite. And while I have a strong aesthetic sense, I am not an elitist. I'm a populist, a democrat— even, I think it's fair to say, a grateful immigrant.

It's funny—I spent most of the sixties in the heart of the East Coast action, at the foot of St. Mark's Place in Manhattan, where the East Village scene bloomed. And I missed it all. Drugs, rebellion, demonstrations—these were luxuries for an immigrant kid still living with his parents in Bronx workers' housing. I got into trouble only once during those years, when I defiantly made an act of symbolic resistance in a class called "Structures." It had become clear to me that much of what was taught at Cooper Union—and, for that matter, at most architecture schools in those days—was about how to build private homes for the wealthy. Go design a Long

Island beach house, we were told in one class. I'd never seen such a thing; I had to take a train out to the Island to figure out what the instructor wanted. Then, in "Structures," we were told to draw a suburban house. I had no interest in building a suburban home, and was pretty certain I'd never design one. "Let me draw another type of building," I begged my instructor, but he told me in no uncertain terms to follow the assignment. I didn't. Instead, I turned in an elaborate drawing of Pier Luigi Nervi's bus terminal near the George Washington Bridge in upper Manhattan, which has one of the most complicated structures of any modern public building. My instructor was not impressed with my insubordination. He gave me a D.

Know where that instructor wound up? Working with Larry Silverstein.

Word went out that the competition organizers would announce a finalist—or perhaps two—at the end of January or in early February.

"Why two?" Nina wondered. "Why make it confusing like that?" Sometimes it felt as if the organizers were making up the rules as they went along. At the same time, it was hard not to be sympathetic, because this competition was unlike any other. The proposals were, for the most part, better and more varied than had been anticipated, and public interest was more intense than anyone could have imagined. The stakes, in all respects, were growing every day. "In our hype-drenched era, a critic will have to risk raising cynical eyebrows with superlatives adequate to the occasion. Let them rise. Let them arch into furious knots. The architects have risen to the occasion. So should we," quoth Herbert Muschamp in *The New York Times*.

A quiet tug-of-war began to play itself out. Major real estate developers came forward to give interviews in which they made it known that it was *they* who ultimately determined what was built in Gotham. The media warned New Yorkers not to get their hopes up too much: "For all the high-minded talk of the allegory and repose in the designs," wrote one *Times* reporter, "commercial considerations will be large and perhaps the leading factors in determining what is built and when." Remember, he noted, this was a competition "to create a land-use plan for the site."

But that's not what the people wanted to hear. They did not want the New York real estate industry or those swayed by backdoor political considerations to decide what would be built on the site. They saw the potential for greatness and authenticity and meaning; they were reveling in the democratic process. They wanted a winner, and they wanted a hand in picking that winner.

CNN, AOL, and local media polled "regular people" to see which proposals the public preferred. In mid-January, the *Times* reported that opinion leaned in favor of three—ours,

Norman Foster's kissing towers, and surprisingly, the design by Peterson Littenberg, which, though fairly uninspired-looking, featured the most park space, with a tree-lined promenade that stretched out over the Hudson.

On January 21, 2003, *The New York Times* ran an editorial that began: "This is a critical time for Lower Manhattan. . . . The closer the time for real, final decisions comes, the more pressure will be brought on the decision makers to think small or bow to the desires of commercial and political interests. . . . One of the two design finalists should certainly be Daniel Libeskind's soaring garden tower and ground-level memorial that uses the slurry wall holding back the Hudson River as a backdrop." No other plan was mentioned.

We kept working madly, exploring the various facets of our scheme and trying to address concerns that had been raised. I've never been one for architectonic fantasies. I wanted to make sure we had a plan that could actually be built.

Larry Silverstein was demanding even more leasable office space. In our original design, the towers were slender. The challenge was to make them bigger but keep them in balance with the site. There's a whole science to office space; formulas determine how many feet should go between elevator core and windows and how space is distributed among offices so that not a single square inch is wasted. While paying attention to these matters, we were concerned about Larry Silverstein's uncompromising demands for yet more office space without regard for the public plazas, parks, memorials, and streets of the master plan.

The Port Authority was worried that we proposed to take the stores out of the underground shopping concourses and raise them to street level. We had done this in order to enliven the streetscape. When the Twin Towers stood, the plazas around them were charmless by day, barren by night; we wanted to fill the streets with bustling life. But the underground commuter shopping mall was a cash cow for the Port Authority, which runs PATH, the commuter line to New Jersey. We had to find a way to respect the Port Authority's interest in maintaining its cash flow while creating lively and pedestrian-oriented street-level retail areas.

Bob Davidson at the Port Authority compared the project to a Rubik's Cube, and he was right. If you changed one detail—made a street six inches wider or narrower—everything else had to change too.

The most daunting challenge was to figure out what to do about the pit, the bathtub. Hardliners—families of victims, including firefighters and police—were adamant about leaving the space open, down to its seventy-foot-deep bedrock bottom. The families were moved by the fact that we proposed to preserve the pit. But resistance was gaining, and we would have to devise compromises that would work for everyone. It would not be easy. Madelyn Wils, who headed the local community board, and other community leaders worried that people would have to walk around a giant depressed (and perhaps depressing) area. Meanwhile, the Port Authority's engineers were concerned about whether they could protect the slurry wall if the bathtub was kept so low; their questions had to be factored in as well.

Forget Rubik's Cube. This was more like surgery in which you have to replace a defective organ while keeping a network of veins and arteries pumping.

Days before the LMDC and Port Authority were to announce the results of the competition, Larry Silverstein showed his true colors. In a nine-page letter to John Whitehead, the LMDC chair, Silverstein announced that he wasn't wild about any of the final designs—but that it didn't really matter, anyway. What mattered, he said, was that, as the recipient of the insurance money for the Twin Towers (he described himself as "the only private source of funds for redevelopment"), he had the sole right to determine what would be built—and what would be vetoed. And he made it clear that if he didn't get his way, he could complicate matters for everyone else.

Copies of Silverstein's letter went to the governors of New York and New Jersey, to New York City mayor Michael Bloomberg, and to officials at the Port Authority. The press got them too.

Here's another thing Larry Silverstein made very clear in his letter: Although this competition was ostensibly to name a master planner for the World Trade Center site, he had already picked Skidmore, Owings & Merrill as *his* master planner. He expected whoever won to work with SOM.

This was ironic for a number of reasons, the most glaring being that SOM had started as one of the seven finalists, but had withdrawn its proposal after the December presentation, presumably to avoid public embarrassment because its submission was so roundly disliked. The firm was quick to insist that it was pulling out to avoid a conflict of interest, since it was already doing business with Silverstein, but nobody was fooled. Why had they entered the competition in the first place?

Why did Silverstein throw in his lot with SOM this way? I still don't know. His letter offended everybody. Bloomberg's office jumped in to object. So did a spokesperson for the Port Authority, as did one for the LMDC. Roland Betts, a driving force on the LMDC board (and a close friend of President George W. Bush), told reporters, "We had a number of consultants looking at all the issues that were raised in that letter and we came to different conclusions than Silverstein."

Silverstein grew quiet for a while after that, but only because he was busy with his lawyers. They were planning a suit against the insurance companies. It seems that Silverstein's policy covered his property to the tune of $3.5 billion in the case of a terrorist incident. But how, exactly, did one define "incident"? Silverstein's theory was that since there were two planes, and each attacked a separate building, there were two separate attacks and he was entitled to $3.5 billion *for each one*. He was demanding $7 billion.

"Do you think he'll get it?" I asked our lawyer, Eddie Hayes.

"Look at it this way," Eddie said. "If only one tower had been hit and collapsed, do you think he would have settled for half of three and a half billion? I don't think so." My lawyer felt Silverstein would fail. But at the time, many people felt he would succeed—in part because Larry Silverstein is used to getting what he wants. I was reminded of the time he took Nina and me out on his sizable yacht. Apparently he had spotted a boat, liked it, wanted it, but felt it was too small. Rather than look for a bigger boat, he bought this one, had it chopped in half, and had an extension stuck into the middle. *Et voilà:* Larry Silverstein gets what he wants.

But not always. He would spend more than a year and would gamble some $100 million in legal fees chasing the $7 billion that he said was his. This time he did not get what he wanted.

February 1, 2003. We got the call: It was now down to two, Studio Daniel Libeskind and THINK Group.

THINK! I was surprised. I'd been expecting Norman Foster's towers to be one of the choices. Perhaps if his towers had not been so massively tall they would have been chosen, but their size scared people, and developers did not want to build so high so soon. In recent weeks, THINK had been positioning itself in the media as the home team, which was definitely a stretch, but a good public relations move. And Frederic Schwartz and Rafael Viñoly were both well connected. Both were good friends of Herbert Muschamp's. I would later learn that Roland Betts had become a loyal supporter of theirs. Even though he was on the board of the LMDC, and presumably open to all the candidates until the final presentations had been made, it is rumored, although it has never been confirmed, that he wrote letters to the business community underscoring his support for THINK.

A few days later, the phone rang. It was Carla Swickerath. "Have you seen the *Times* yet?" she asked. "Get it, get it, *get it*."

It was early in the morning and I wasn't quite awake. Yet.

In the *Times*, it turned out, Herbert Muschamp had offered "an appraisal" of the two finalists. "Taken together as a kind of shotgun diptych," he wrote, "the two designs . . . illustrate the confusion of a nation torn between the conflicting impulses of war and peace." *Shotgun diptych?*

"Daniel Libeskind's project for the World Trade Center site is a startlingly aggressive tour de force, a war memorial to a looming conflict that has scarcely begun. The THINK team's proposal, on the other hand, offers an image of peacetime aspirations so idealistic as to seem nearly unrealizable.

"While no pacifist, as a modern-day New Yorker I would like to think my way to a place beyond armed combat. . . . [The THINK design] is an act of metamorphosis. It transforms our collective memories of the Twin Towers into a soaring affirmation of American values."

What? What insanity was this? After the Winter Garden presentations, Muschamp had written: "Studio Daniel Libeskind. If you are looking for the marvelous, here's where you will find it." And then there had been that *Times* editorial, which, if he had not written it himself, he most certainly had signed off on. How had we, in the course of two weeks, gone from a "soaring" design to an "aggressive . . . war memorial"?

This was bizarre. What did Muschamp see when he looked at the skeletal towers of the "World Cultural Center" proposed by THINK? In that plan, the museum, performing arts center, and conference center were suspended between the two towers, floating modules. On the northern tower, the module was to be connected at the point where the plane slammed into the North Tower on 9/11. And on the southern tower, the module was to be connected at the spot where the plane had shot into the South Tower. Whether people liked the design or not, I had a hard time seeing how it offered an image of "peacetime aspirations so idealistic as to seem nearly unrealizable."

I went back to reading. Muschamp was not remotely finished. He derided my attempt as a "predictably kitsch result." Whoa. That's as low a blow as you can deliver in architecture criticism—to call something kitsch. You can say a design is ugly. That it is impractical. You can even say it's a rip-off of another design. But don't ever call it kitsch.

(1.) THE HEART AND THE SOUL:
MEMORY FOUNDATIONS

MEMORIAL SITE EXPOSES
<u>GROUND ZERO</u>
ALL THE WAY DOWN TO THE
<u>BEDROCK FOUNDATIONS.</u>

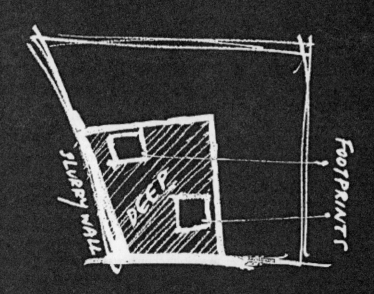

REVEALING THE HEROIC FOUNDATIONS
OF DEMOCRACY FOR ALL TO SEE.

Here is how Muschamp concluded his "appraisal": "The spaces [THINK] proposes for memorial observance could be as eloquent as a cathedral's. But they would be enclosed with the Enlightenment framework that has stabilized this country since birth. From mourning, it would build towers of learning. They would lift us high above the level of feudal superstition in which our enemies remain mired."

Towers of learning? The phrase sounded as if it had been lifted from Stalinist literature! What was the man eating for breakfast?

The next day, as Nina, holding Rachel by the hand, walked into the Winter Garden, a *Los Angeles Times* reporter who was writing a story about me approached her. "So," the reporter said, "what did you think of Muschamp's attack?"

Nina laughed. "My husband is more ecumenical than I am. I'd like to kill him," she said, referring to Muschamp.

Her offhand comment appeared in the next day's L.A. *Times*, and was picked up by a dozen other papers.

Months later, after we won the competition, Nina persuaded Muschamp to join us for a fence-mending session at the Four Seasons Hotel in New York. She apologized profusely to him for her wisecrack, but her effort was not very successful. Muschamp was openly confrontational and dismissive. His main objection seemed to be to the names I'd given the elements of the plan—Park of Heroes, Wedge of Light. And he hated the explicit references to the symbols of the United States—the Statue of Liberty and 1776—which

Ⓔ. SEPTEMBER II MATRIX

HEROES LINES
TO GROUND ZERO

he considered right-wing and jingoistic. I tried to talk to him about this, but he wasn't interested.

"But earlier you loved all this," Nina told him. "You said so in the paper. Our proposal hasn't changed. Our words haven't changed. Daniel hasn't changed. What made you change your mind?"

"Back in December, you were still one of seven finalists," Muschamp replied coldly. "Then you became one of two. That changed everything."

I suddenly understood. It wasn't about which scheme was best. Evidently, Muschamp wanted to handpick from his inner circle.

While Herbert Muschamp had switched alliances mid-coverage, William Neuman, a reporter at the *New York Post*, was an attack dog from the start. My favorite moment with the *Post* came when I discovered that Neuman had tracked down my sister to see if we'd *really* come to the United States by boat, or if it was all a public relations stunt. Why was the *Post* so savage about us and our plan? I have no idea. But the attacks never let up.

There was no time to worry about it, though. We had to focus our plans. So much to do, so much to study—density, phasing, costs, feasibility. New calculations, drawings, a host of alterations. Nina mobilized us as if we were preparing to cross the Rubicon. She made a radical decision: she called all our clients around the world, asked for their understanding, and postponed every deadline. Each client responded by agreeing, and our entire office delved

③ WEDGE OF LIGHT / PARK OF HEROES

SUNLIGHT ON SEPTEMBER 11
MARKING THE PRECISE
TIME OF THE EVENT.

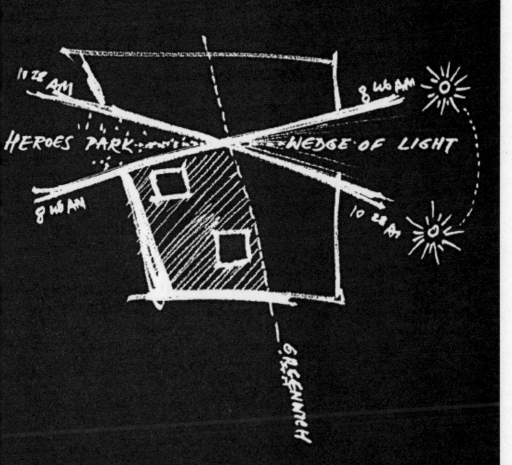

into the work with intensity and passion. Nina took what little money we had and poured it into the effort.

On both sides of the Atlantic, we began cleaning up: we shelved every model, rolled up every drawing, and closed every computer file that was not related to the WTC. The architects were split into groups, each with a leader, its own office, and a specific task to complete. To coordinate all efforts, Nina scheduled daily meetings with the group leaders, and in the meantime she and I sprinted from room to room, day and night, overseeing elevator core studies, subway vent analyses, and a dizzying array of newfangled security devices and technologies.

We decided to concentrate on the concerns of the Port Authority, because the more we had worked on the project, the more we understood how much of what was important in rebuilding lower Manhattan lay underground. The WTC site is at the tip of Manhattan, where so much squeezes together and converges. Electricity lines, elevator cores, transportation. Oh, the transportation! The commuter lines, where tens of thousands of passengers disembark every day from Jersey. The 1, 2, 3, 4, 5, 6, 9, A, C, E, J, M, N, Q, R, W, and Z lines of the New York subway. The Brooklyn Battery Tunnel. The Holland Tunnel. The Brooklyn Bridge. These are the lifelines of the city, and changing anything costs billions of dollars.

In the competition, we watched the Port Authority officials were sometimes given short shrift by our fellow architects. They're not glamour guys, they're infrastructure guys—transportation, structural, and material engineers. But

(4.) CULTURE AT HEART :
PROTECTIVE FILTER AND OPEN
ACCESS TO HALLOWED GROUND

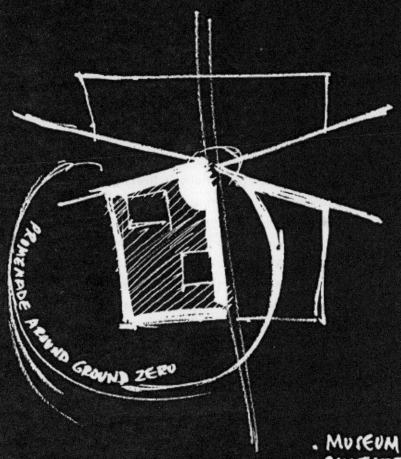

- MUSEUM
- CULTURE
- PROMENADE

only a fool ignores the Port Authority people, who are world-class experts on these immense projects.

I knew that we had better learn as much as we could from them, as quickly as possible.

I was taken on a walk by some Port Authority officials through the empty tubes of the PATH trains. Out we went, way out, under the Hudson. What's there is mind-boggling—a whole city, seven stories high, an underwater cathedral that the public never sees. There is so much to protect in lower Manhattan. The Port Authority said: You can't park tourist buses under the new towers, because any of them could be packed with explosives. So where do you park them that is out of sight and secure? How do you safely truck supplies in under the new towers? Every conundrum contained another ten within.

Most important, how do we make sure, in the process of doing all this construction, that we don't undermine the stability of the remaining foundation at Ground Zero? There, with the slurry wall holding back the Hudson, everything is in constant flux. As I sit here typing, and as you sit there reading, someone is checking millimeter shifts in the structure to ensure that everything is working properly.

We may not have had Herbert Muschamp or the *New York Post* in our corner, but we did have Edward W. Hayes. In New York, you can't do much better than that.

Eddie Hayes is a legend in the city, one of those human

⑤ LIFE VICTORIOUS / SKYLINE

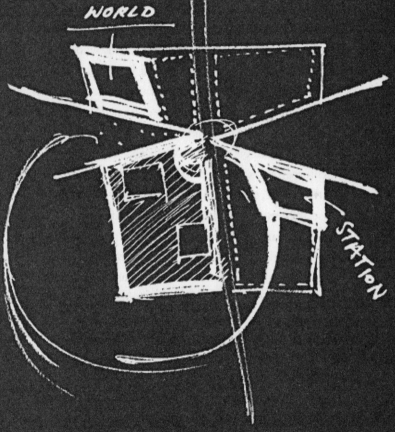

VERTICAL GARDENS OF THE WORLD

STATION

REASSERTING THE SKYLINE

1776 ft

connectors who knows everyone from the governor on down. When Tom Wolfe wrote *The Bonfire of the Vanities*, not only did he model one of his greatest characters on Hayes—the New Yawk–tawkin' defense lawyer Tommy Killian—he actually dedicated the book to him: "Doffing his hat, the author dedicates this book to COUNSELOR EDDIE HAYES, who walked among the flames, pointing at the lurid lights." Hayes understands New York. He's a classic New Yorker: fast, opinionated, loyal, rough but slick, angry but huge of heart.

If you saw us together you might not recognize how much we have in common, but it's a lot. We both grew up working-class, me in the Bronx, Eddie in Queens. His mother wrapped packages at Macy's; mine worked in sweatshops. We both developed a love of art (Eddie famously handled the Andy Warhol Estate). And we both love Nina—or as Ed puts it, "I like him okay, but I *really* like her." We started out as friends, but when Eddie officially became our lawyer, he told someone, "Nina manages me better than any other client I've ever had, except for a couple of gangsters years ago." That is high praise coming from Ed Hayes.

Our friend Victoria Newhouse, who had written about the Berlin Jewish Museum in her book *Towards a New Museum*, brought Ed and me together over dinner. "I knew you'd like each other," she said at the end of the dinner, and she was right; we were immediately friends. As we parted that night, Ed told me, "Daniel, go out tomorrow and buy a copy of Governor Pataki's autobiography and read it. You gotta know how The Guy thinks."

The Guy—that's what Ed calls his old friend the governor of New York. I bought the book the next day, and sat down and read it. I realized what Ed Hayes wanted me to see— amazingly, I had a lot in common with George Pataki too. The differences were obvious: Pataki is a Republican (a progressive one), owns substantial property, and was born and raised upstate, in Peekskill. But his parents had immigrated, from Hungary, and they struggled, and Pataki is a self-made man. There was another similarity, an odd one: Eastern and Central Europeans have a fondness for taking photos of their children posed in front of haystacks; my parents did it, and so, apparently, did Pataki's. The next time I saw Ed Hayes, I handed him my version of the photo, and he burst out laughing. It was identical to a photo in Pataki's book. "Wow," he said. "I knew you and The Guy were similar. I just didn't realize you grew up in the same damn town."

When Governor Pataki went to view the models on display at the Winter Garden, Ed Hayes went with him. And he showed Pataki, who had grown up by the Hudson, how my plan relates to the water, to the Hudson and New York Harbor. "See how the spiral of buildings talks to the water, and reaches out to the Statue of Liberty?" And Eddie gave The Guy a copy of my haystack portrait.

Never before were the media so interested in the lives of architects. Shortly before the conclusion of the competition,

The Wall Street Journal published a damaging page-one story about Rafael Viñoly, raising questions about his possible past involvement with the military junta in Argentina, where Viñoly started as an architect. In interviews—in newspapers, on the *Today* show—Viñoly had presented himself as a political refugee forced to flee his home.

There was no love lost between the THINK Group and Studio Daniel Libeskind. Schwartz and Viñoly had made their antipathy clear from the start, and now they were becoming downright ugly. Viñoly referred in the press to the bathtub as a "death pit." I responded by saying that his towers looked like skeletons. I also pointed out that the group's name was disturbing—THINK. Why the capitals? It seemed Orwellian, scary.

What confused me most was the fact that THINK's proposal was budgeted at three times the amount of our plan—and yet cost never appeared as a factor in anyone's decision making. What's more, the THINK phasing seemed impossible. Before any functioning buildings could be erected, two enormous steel-frame structures would have to be put up. Once they were up, engineers would then face the challenge of suspending floating modules between the structures, and during the lengthy time it would take to erect the gigantic frames and secure the modules to them, the site would be rendered unusable and off-limits. It didn't make any sense. And yet no one seemed bothered by the impracticality.

Was anyone really paying attention, I wondered.

As the deadline approached, our indomitable architects were bringing their sleeping bags to the office so they could crash under their desks between shifts. The model builders pulled all-nighters. Nina and I had been shuttling between Berlin and New York, but now we settled into a hotel for the long haul. When we were finished, our team of twenty-five young architects emerged red-eyed and exhausted, not having seen their families—or sunlight—for weeks. They looked like newts, their skin tender and gray-green. It is hard to find the words to express how proud we were of them; as Ed Hayes would say, they'd busted their balls to complete the proposal.

On February 25, two days before the winner was to be announced, things went suddenly quiet. The finalists, Studio Libeskind and THINK, were to make their presentations that evening to the Selection Committee. But something—everything—felt wrong to Nina. She had been calling Ed Hayes regularly, because no one understood the lay of New York better than he. Ed was her interpreter. And her friend. Now she phoned him, concerned.

"Something's wrong," she told him. "I can feel it."

"You're out of your fucking mind," Eddie replied. "Relax, Nina."

She was adamant. "Eddie, I've been in politics all my life. I know the signs. Things are *too* quiet."

Eddie promised to investigate.

The Selection Committee met with us at six p.m. It was

hard to get the members' attention. They were distracted, reluctant to make eye contact.

Nina turned to the LMDC's Andrew Winters and asked, "Are we still in?"

"Yeah, yeah, don't worry, you're still in," he said, but he looked pale and unconvincing.

She turned to Quentin Brathwaite of the Port Authority. "Are we still in this competition?"

"Yeah, yeah, don't worry," he answered, but he looked no more convincing than Andrew.

Viñoly was scheduled to appear at seven p.m., after our presentation, but we were still there when he cruised in more than thirty minutes late. He didn't seem anxious at all. Which was understandable in light of what we later learned. Roland Betts, who headed the LMDC Site Planning Committee, had called a meeting earlier in the day, and the committee had agreed to vote for THINK. This paved the way for the group's selection.

The presentations had been a sham. And Viñoly had known it.

The next morning, Nina called Ed again. "Seen the paper yet?" she asked.

"No," he said. "It's seven-thirty, I just into my office."

"We lost."

"You're out of your mind," Eddie said.

"You said that last night. Go look at your paper."

The committee had voted for THINK's plan for Ground

Zero. The words were emblazoned on the front page of *The New York Times*.

Here's Eddie's version of what happened next: "And so I'm sitting there, talking to Nina and looking at the paper, and I'm thinking, Holy whatever! They lost! And I think to myself, You know it's ridiculous that Eddie Hayes is going to push The Guy on something like this, but it's me or nobody. I've seen the model. I know the plans. I know the man. I know Libeskind's the right guy for this. So I call The Guy, and within a couple of minutes, The Guy calls me back."

Governor Pataki said to Ed Hayes, "What am I going to do? I don't think I agree with the committee, but I picked these people."

And Eddie said, "This project will define your legacy, as much as anything you've done. You gotta do whatever you think is right, whatever you think is best."

A final presentation was to be made that very day to Governor Pataki and Mayor Bloomberg, before the official decision was announced. Roland Betts was to present the proposals to the governor and the mayor, but there was a change of plans. The governor asked that the architects present their own proposals. At noon, Alexander Garvin, vice-president for planning, design, and development for the LMDC, phoned. "Can you get here by one o'clock?" he said. He sounded urgent.

We scrambled. Nina and I were in a taxi, speeding along the FDR Drive on our way to the LMDC offices, when Eddie called. "I spoke with The Guy."

"Did you ask him to support us?"

"No."

"*No?*"

"No, I just told him he has to do what he thinks is right, and then he said—"

Nothing. The phone cut out. We were at a part of the highway where phones go dead. We never got Ed back.

At the LMDC, we were up first. "You have thirty minutes with the governor and the mayor," Andrew Winters told us.

Governor Pataki and Mayor Bloomberg came into the appointed conference room and greeted us.

"Governor and Mayor," I said, "I know you are both busy men, and if I can't explain it to you in five minutes, it's probably not worth building anyway." I showed Pataki and Bloomberg key conceptual plans and the very beautiful models our staff had built, and explained the phasing for the master plan. And that was all it took. For the next twenty-five minutes, the governor and the mayor circled the model, asking knowledgeable and practical questions. The governor, closing one eye, peered across the model from the south as if imagining what the actual site might one day look like from the deck of an approaching ship.

The governor and the mayor left the room to go next door for Viñoly's presentation. Nina and I felt that we had represented our proposal well. We had argued its merits as eloquently as we could, and between the two of us had left nothing out. But we had to stay and wait in case there were further questions. The wait was excruciating.

We later learned that when Viñoly walked in for his presentation, he was confident he had won. Spotting one of our models as he passed by our conference room, he turned to our associate Stefan Blach and said quietly, "You might as well just rip that model up now, no?" And then he smiled. The press often referred to Viñoly's charm, but I'm afraid my group didn't see a lot of it.

Yet it wasn't charm, or lack of it, that was decisive for Governor Pataki and Mayor Bloomberg. In the end, I'm told, the decision was both visceral and pragmatic. There were two very different choices before them. THINK was proposing a megastructure that would present a decade-long headache to erect and an eternal reminder of the destroyed towers. Our plan was diversified, so it could be built in pieces, a building at a time, over time.

After Viñoly's final presentation, the governor and the mayor talked between themselves, then joined John Whitehead, Roland Betts, and other officials gathered around a table in a conference room. Pataki told the committee members that he was overruling them. He wanted something both visionary and realistic, and my plan was the only one that could actually be built. When some members tried to argue, the governor turned to the mayor. "Mike, I've got a meeting in midtown in fifteen minutes," he said. "Can you explain to them why I picked Libeskind?"

Of course, we didn't know any of this. By then we had been told to go, and so we had returned to our hotel room to wait. Nina was despondent, convinced that the governor would allow the committee to choose THINK. I sat calmly reading a book by the contemporary thinker Emmanuel Levinas, and attempted to be philosophical. "Nina," I said, "what it taught us was worth the effort in itself." She shot me a look. It had cost us so much—in money, time, strength, patience, will, heart, not to mention the heroic efforts of our team—and now it seemed as if it had all been for naught. Our son Lev had arrived in New York from Tel Aviv, and when he called, I could hear the disappointment in Nina's voice. "We lost, okay? There is nothing we can do about it—it's over. I'm packing the bags."

Then the phone rang again. Nina picked it up, and her face went white. She held the phone out to me and said, "It's John Whitehead. . . ."

I took it, bracing myself for the standard consolation speech from the chairman.

And then I heard the words: "Mr. Libeskind, you've won!" I could feel the blood rush to my head. Stuttering, I thanked the chairman and flashed Nina a V sign. Then I hung up and gave her a big kiss.

The next day *The New York Times* ran a photo of me on page one. All you could see was my head, surrounded by an ocean of photographers and reporters. Nina—who knows where she was? We lost each other at the press conference.

The explosion of interest was overwhelming, the euphoria intense. It was February 27, 2003, and the course of my life had been altered forever.

Exhausted but too exhilarated to stay in our hotel room, we took our staff and friends to the bar of the Ritz-Carlton at Battery Park, which offers a magical, sweeping view of New York Harbor and the Statue of Liberty.

"We're moving to New York!" I said.

Ed Hayes arrived, in a custom-tailored English suit and a pink silk tie. He looked like a million bucks. "I just got off the phone with The Guy," Eddie said. "He told me to tell you it was the haystack that did it in the end."

Eddie's a teetotaler; he never drinks. So we raised a glass on his behalf.

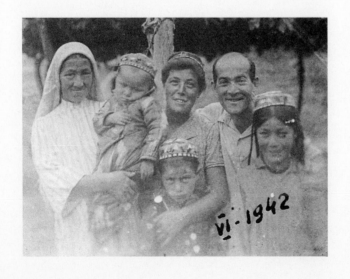

the
invisible

What attracts people to something? There's no *reason*
we are drawn to a flower, or a face, or the beauty of a
particular landscape. Or even to something that isn't
necessarily pretty to look at—the ruins of an ancient
temple, for example. Why does a particular city speak
to us in a special way? And why do cities take root in
particular spots? Berlin, for example, is in the sizable
province of Brandenburg, Germany. Now the capital of
a united country, Berlin was once a small town in the
heart of Prussia, and long before that, Slavic and Ger-
manic tribes wrestled over it. It was—is—in the middle
of nowhere. Yes, it is situated on the banks of the Spree,

but the river moves on, and the city stays behind. When did someone decide, "This is the spot, this is where we stay?" And what was it about that spot that made people feel this was indeed where they should settle? This was their destiny.

What makes a place or a building feel right? It's more than a human force at work. Maybe there is something divine involved, though that word makes people nervous. But whatever you call it, I am not alone in feeling that much of what I do has to do with the Invisible.

I want to tell you a story with a spooky ending.

At one time, the Victoria and Albert Museum in London was the jewel in the crown of London's network of museums. It is the world's greatest museum of decorative arts, boasting seven miles of exhibition space, four million objects (metalwork, textiles, furniture, you name it) dating as far back as between two thousand and five thousand years in antiquity, depending on whom you believe. From the start, the museum had a fussy air. Its first director was Sir Henry Cole, a very pragmatic Victorian architect, as well as a dedicated watercolorist. When the doors to the museum first opened in 1857, Cole declared that he intended it to be a "schoolroom for everyone." An admirable intention, but in today's terms, not all that sexy.

From a fussy start, the museum grew more grandmotherly and musty, so much so that by 1996, the directors and board of trustees were alarmed. A great institution was fast fading into neglect and decay. What could be done to save it? They turned, as museum directors and board members often do, to architects and asked, "What do you see?"

After spending much time wandering around the haute Victorian buildings near Cromwell Road in South Kensington, so near to Harrods—the Imperial College, the Natural History Museum, the Royal Albert Hall—I had an immediate sense of what was needed: a crystalline spiral that would rise nine stories in one dazzling continuous piece, providing unprecedented spaces and drama. This unexpected structure would make us experience London in a new way. In terms of its engineering, the spiral (which would come to be known as, yes, the Spiral) was a unique innovation, without a single curve, a form whose every wall interlocked with another wall and was self-supported. If unfolded and set end to end, the walls of the Spiral would be equal in length to Exhibition Road, the street on which the Spiral extension sits. This, I felt strongly, was a fitting complement to a building that celebrated Britain's rich heritage of craft techniques, building technology, and the decorative arts, as exemplified by the marvelous William Morris and Owen Jones.

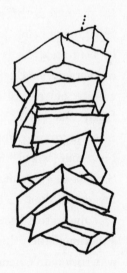

Oh! said the director. If this spiral was built, it could achieve "the status of a national icon, as the Eiffel Tower does for Paris and the Empire State Building does for New York."

But oh! the ensuing fuss. London is a conservative town, and my suggestion was seen by a few as an act of aggression. The former editor of *The Times* of London, William Rees-Mogg, called it "an insult to everything the museum stands for," and warned that its construction would be "a disaster for the Victoria and Albert Museum in particular and for civilization in general." (I do wish my mother were here to see me pose a threat to all of civilization.) Rees-Mogg accused me of being deconstructive. "What is deconstructive?" he continued. "It is the tearing down of the old culture of scholarship, truth, beauty, reason and order because that culture of the Enlightenment is seen as having failed. Sartre, Mao, and Libeskind stand for the belief that a great new epuration through barbarism is the only way to the brave new world." Well, I didn't mind being compared to Sartre—he's a great thinker. But Mao—I never had the following of Mao!

I argued that I was not a deconstructivist; I believe in construction. When the Victorians built the museum 150 years ago, they didn't erect what had been in fashion 150 years before that, in the Georgian era. The Victorians were brave and radical, shocking even. They built a contemporary building. I was proposing the same. Look at the exterior walls of the museum, I said. There you will find statues of visionaries and risk takers—Christopher Wren, John Barry, and John Soane.

They may have had their eccentricities, but they were not fuddy-duddies. By looking backward, you will condemn London to a life of nostalgia and nothing more, I said.

My detractors fought back. "What does the word *harmony* mean to you?" they demanded. They wanted to know how the crystalline spiral, clad in special ceramic tile, fit harmoniously beside this lovely if dowdy old museum.

The differences, I replied, were harmonic. The harmonies of Mozart differ from the harmonies of Bach, which differ from the harmonies of Copland, which differ from the harmonies of any number of contemporary composers. And yet they all can—and do—appear on the same musical program. People are more open-minded than is often supposed. Building is dynamic. Streetscapes are meant to change. Great food, great wine, great movies, great books incite new thoughts, new desires. When it was founded, the V&A was to be a contemporary museum of design; its galleries were meant to inspire artists and designers, and to focus not on the past but on the new: novel Ferraris, the fashions of Vivienne Westwood, the latest in photography.

In time, I knew I had convinced most of the under-forty set. But the biggest hurdle lay before me: in order to proceed with my plan, the museum directors needed approval from English Heritage, a commission created to preserve and protect buildings of historical interest. This august body had veto power over the Spiral.

I know certain things about human nature. I know that people want buildings to affirm their own illusions, and that when a building reflects a new angle of reality, or an entirely new view, it can feel disturbing. Especially if it doesn't affirm comfortable, familiar thoughts about the world. And yet the world is not that stable mass supported by four elephants on a turtle's back, as described in Hindu mythology. It is more, I think, as Rilke described it—a place of fluctuation, rotating in a cosmic space. In other words, it changes.

In early 1997, I attended an intensely dramatic eight-a.m. meeting with the commissioners of English Heritage. Their names and titles had a Shakespearean ring—lords, ladies, barons, dukes, sirs. Which century had I entered? The head of the commission was Sir Jocelyn Stevens, a former minister in the Thatcher government. It was a very intimidating group. I composed myself and began my presentation by paraphrasing Oscar Wilde: "Only an idiot can be brilliant at breakfast," I said. The commissioners burst into laughter, and a lord dropped his croissant.

I reminded the commissioners about the spectacular Crystal Palace, which had been seen as a triumph when it was erected in time for the Great Exhibition of 1851 in London, and whose exhibits formed the basis of the V&A collection. An iron leviathan covered in more than a million square feet of glass, it was an awe-inspiring, empire-building showcase. The Spiral, I implied, could be a latter-day Crystal Palace.

To the amazement of many, we won the commission's approval. And in fact, English Heritage proclaimed to all London that perhaps the commission wasn't quite as old-fashioned as was thought. The group took out an ad in the

London papers, with the headline "As Approved by the Old Fuddy-Duddies at English Heritage," and below was a picture of the Spiral, placed elegantly, rightly, in the courtyard of the V&A, overlooking Exhibition Road.

When the battles were over, a curator took me aside. "Mr. Libeskind," she said, "I'd like to show you something I'm sure you haven't seen before."

In a back room of the museum was a small sketch, which I most definitely had not seen before. It was a very pretty thing, depicting the earliest of the V&A buildings—with a spiral construction next to it. The spiral wasn't precisely the same as the one I had designed, but it was a spiral nonetheless, and in precisely the same spot.

"I'm not sure I understand this," I said, feeling a little goofy in my confusion.

"Sir Henry Cole sketched it," the curator told me. "After the building opened."

I was still flummoxed. How could Henry Cole have come up with this image, I asked. He was such a practical, schoolmarmish man.

"I have no idea," she said. "It's completely out of character for him—but he did draw it."

Why did he draw it? Is it possible that some force dictated this precise shape? For some reason, a spiral seems to belong right there. And that knowledge came to Henry Cole. And it came to me. And perhaps it has come to many others in the intervening years. I'd like to think so.

Back in the 1940s, a number of leading scientists were

sent questionnaires by a French psychologist who was trying to understand more about the minds of scientists. When you think deeply, they were asked, do you think in numbers, words, or images? Albert Einstein wrote back: None of them. When it comes to the ultimate recesses of the mind, he said, my thoughts are simply a coordination of muscular *feelings*. Now, I'm no Einstein, but I know what he's saying. When the big thoughts wash over me, they feel like premonitions filled with desire and longing. I can't sustain the feeling for long, nor can I control when it arises.

Here's what is both somewhat sad and a bit funny: Had I spotted Sir Henry Cole's sketch of the spiral earlier, I probably wouldn't have designed one for that spot. The idea would not have seemed original or fresh.

Here's what's also sad, if somewhat funny: Once the sketch was shown to me, I showed it to some of the project's more vociferous critics, and it instantly began to dispel their objections. Because oh! if *Sir Henry* saw it that way . . .

A German newspaper has written that I must have psychic powers, or that if I'm not psychic, then at least I have powers of divination. I'd like to claim them, but I can't. This is how the rumor started: Construction was under way on the Felix Nussbaum Museum in Osnabrück. I had sited the unusually shaped building in a very exact way, topographically.

I wanted one side of the museum to face Berlin, another Rome (Osnabrück is one of the oldest Catholic towns in northern Germany), a third Hamburg—three cities where Nussbaum had studied art—and the fourth the concentration camp where he was murdered.

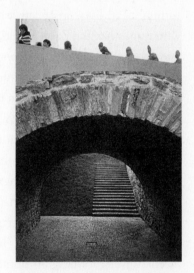

One day, a bulldozer that was clearing the way to the museum's front entrance ran into something. It turned out to be an old bridge. Work stopped until archaeologists could be brought in to inspect the bridge. When they saw it, they were excited to determine that the bridge had been built in the seventeenth century; it was one of the oldest intact bridges in Germany.

"What do we do?" asked the museum director. "We can't move it, and we can't build over it." We didn't have to. The ancient bridge was oriented within one degree—one degree!—of the front entrance. It was as if it had been waiting more than three centuries for the museum to be built. We built a perforated metal bridge directly over it, and that is how one now enters the museum.

I have many stories like this. Indulge me with just one more, because it happened only weeks ago, and my mind keeps returning to it. I was in Milan, where, as part of a consortium with Arata Isozaki, Zaha Hadid, and Pier Paolo Maggiora, I had won the commission to redevelop the historic fairgrounds. Milan has long been one of the leading adventurous design centers of the world, and what is envisioned for the fairgrounds is a bold, beautiful complex of residences and offices, and institutional and cultural centers embracing a vast park space. I am the master planner of the site, as well as the architect of some of the buildings. I have already designed one of the three skyscrapers. Its shape creates a sheltered public space on the ground, rising vertically and then arching gently over the plaza. The tower is like a keystone to the two adjacent towers, forming an implied open-air dome as in the city's Galleria Vittorio Emanuele.

During a break in the meetings related to the project (there are always endless meetings), I slipped away to the Castello Sforzesco, one of Milan's landmarks. It houses a number of galleries, and in one is Michelangelo's unfinished final work, the Pietà Rondanini. What an extraordinary sculpture. Unlike the more polished, seated Pietà in St. Peter's in Rome, this sculpture is powerfully, painfully raw. Mary stands and carries the lifeless body of her son (to whom Michelangelo has given his own features). The artist worked on the sculpture until a few days before he died in 1564.

I have studied the front of this sculpture many times before: the sorrow in Mary's face, the way Jesus' once strong legs now buckle under the weight of his body. But on this visit, something drew me to the back of the sculpture. Because of the way it is positioned, it's not easy to see the rear, and I had to obtain special permission to step behind and look. Once there, I understood what I was looking for. The curve of Mary's back was identical—identical!—to the arching curve of the tower building I had designed for Milan.

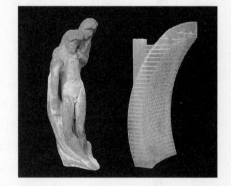

What dictated that beautiful but peculiar shape? You may argue that it's all coincidence, and I am enough of a rationalist to shrug and admit you may be right. But I cannot shake the sense that something else was compelling me to draw the shape in the first place, and to seek it out as well.

I am eager for the Milan fairgrounds buildings to be finished, because until a building is completed you can never really know what it will be like. People think they get to know buildings by studying drawings, models, or renderings, but you must experience a building with your whole body and all your senses before you can fully understand how it works. You can know in advance a building's dimensions; you can know what materials will be used to make it real. But you will not know its soul until it reveals itself to you.

It's the same with music. When people listen to music, they don't hear horsehair rubbing on a gut string, or little wooden mallets hitting a piece of metal; they hear a violin or a piano. And while you can provide the chords and specify the vibrations, *the music is elsewhere*. Between the technique and the art is a mystery.

I realize only now that when my father walked around Lodz after the war, he was comforted—not unnerved—by the ghosts and invisible shadows of his lost city. The spirits of Lodz kept him company. Every week, the two of us would head for the Jewish cemetery, where a line of bullet holes running along the northern wall indicated where victims of the Nazis had been lined up and shot. In front of the wall, stretching some distance, was a field of newly turned earth, and below were the bodies of thousands of Jews without tombstones. Together we faced the Sisyphean task of cleaning up and restoring the tombs of relatives and friends. This was the biggest Jewish cemetery in Europe, but there was no one left to care for the graves. My father and I did what little we could to make the place neat and orderly again. We did it as if to spite the historical odds, as if to prove that memory is more powerful than the combined force of human destructiveness and natural decay.

When I first moved to Berlin, I visited the huge Jewish

cemetery in Weissensee, then in East Berlin, which, like the one in Lodz, was in a state of disrepair. Stepping over the broken stones, and along the unweeded paths, I had an overwhelming urge to stay and clear out the vegetation, and polish the tombstones, and honor the dead by placing small stones on their graves—but I couldn't. There were too many of them.

There is a sickness known as Jerusalem syndrome, which strikes primarily in the Old City. The victim, usually visiting for the first time, begins to hear voices and perhaps suffer from religious delusions, and then goes mad. The Israeli government has even set up a psychiatric ward for those afflicted by this odd disorder. It is the mingling of ancient ghostliness and modern holiness that sickens those who suffer from the syndrome. Every step they take lands in a footprint left long ago, and caught up in the city's historical choreography, they become entranced by its architecture and fall under the delusion they are angels, prophets, or saints.

Lately I've been working with a feng shui master, in connection with a media center I am building for the City University of Hong Kong. It has been a fascinating experience. When completed, the center will be one of the most high-tech buildings in Hong Kong—but the ancient art of feng shui will have been central to its design. That is the case too with Norman Foster's Hongkong and Shanghai bank tower, that most expensive building in Hong Kong. Foster had to reposition escalators carefully so that they were parallel rather than perpendicular to the street, in order to prevent wealth from flowing out of the building. Principles of feng shui also dictated that main structural supports be inverted to look like M's instead of W's.

Feng shui may strike some as a pseudo-science, and I confess that I suspect the basic spirit of the City University building would not have been significantly altered if I had left it red as originally intended. But under feng shui, too much red is thought to lead to arguments. (Too much black is thought to be draining.) I made other adjustments: I altered some of the angles of the building to ensure that they were properly attuned to the ancient spirits. I learned many things working with the feng shui master, and I saw that many of the beliefs have a basis in empirical reality. Feng shui is all about how a structure relates to water, to views—how a building is oriented in the world. And that is something all architects must understand and respect.

That's exactly what Vitruvius tried to get across some two thousand years ago. Marcus Vitruvius Pollio was a Roman architect, and the author of the earliest-known architectural treatise. His *De Architectura*, written in the first century B.C.E., was an essential textbook well into Renaissance times. Much of what he wrote about was practical—construction methods, materials, theories of proportions in buildings. But embedded in the practical was a discussion of more subtle and mystical concerns. He spoke of divination, and how important it is to be mindful of omens, as well as natural phenomena such as the flight of birds, the movement of wind and light. He advised architects to become expert in the flight patterns of birds, because by studying their flight patterns one can learn a lot about what is happening on the ground. It's all connected.

Just before I graduated from Cooper Union, I won a scholarship to travel around the United States to study Frank Lloyd Wright's architecture. Two other students, another architect and an artist, also won scholarships. The concept behind the scholarships was wonderful; the money was not. Nina and I had just married, so for our honeymoon, we pooled our money with the other students and together bought plane tickets to Chicago. We rented a station wagon there, then drove to St. Louis, explored Eero Saarinen's soaring Gateway Arch, and started out on our great American road trip.

I don't travel with a camera; I travel with a sketchbook. I filled sketchbook after sketchbook, trying to capture the lyricism of America and its sublime grandeur. I sketched the desert, the rocks of New Mexico, the canyons of Arizona, the mushroom columns of Wright's Johnson Wax building in Wisconsin, and the mountains of Colorado. We couldn't afford motels every night, so sometimes we slept in the car or in all-night movie theaters. We visited almost every building of Wright's. As we crossed mountains and deserts, for the first time I understood the vastness of America and its majesty. And for the first time too, I understood Vitruvius.

In North America, nature hovers over man, and it is this,

I think, that the American architect too often forgets. Sometimes American architecture seems to have gotten stuck in skyscraper typology. But it must continue to evolve into something new, because America, as is often said, keeps changing.

We take for granted the shapes that define us: the shape of a window, the shape of a piece of land, the very particular shape of Manhattan and the World Trade Center site. An elongated landmass, pinched between two rivers: Manhattan's shape probably has more to do with its impact on America's architecture than any building ever could have.

Ignore the spiritual history and reality of your country at your own peril. That's the message I've always taken from Stanley Kubrick's film *The Shining*. I love that movie—Jack Nicholson and Shelley Duvall up in that giant, fading resort in the Rockies. People have their own interpretations of the movie, but to me it's about architecture, and the fact that woven into the fabric of every building is a past, and spirits, and a spiritual reality, and if you try to resist their force, *something terrible* will happen to you. I've been haunted by the movie since the events of 9/11. The repeated, deadly visions of the pretty twin girls have struck me as visions of the Twin Towers themselves.

When I was in high school at Bronx Science, I heard of a kid who had toured the Civil War battlefields at Gettysburg and found them still strewn with shot. I've since wandered the fields there—they have been picked clean by now—but no one has been able to wipe out the painful past. It is a potent force that hovers over what appears to be ordinary land: more than 45,000 men were killed or wounded in those fields in three days. It's not difficult to understand why a sense of history is so palpable there. But there are other places where I become keenly aware of a historical spirit, and I don't necessarily know why, because the specific events may have been lost over time. For all the newness of California, I constantly feel a Native American presence when I'm there. The first time I experienced it I was teaching at UCLA, in the middle of Los Angeles. I looked out the window at the idyllic scene and suddenly felt, "An Indian mound is here." I could sense it. It wasn't ghosts, or anything so trite. It was a powerful sensation that the openness before me had been created by something—something I could never really know or name, yet something to be aware of and care for.

There is a bolter—a guy who bolts steel—who has been working on the museum extension in Denver for some time now. He gave up his job in Florida after he saw pictures of the plans for the building; he knew he had to work on it. He was a high-paid crane operator, but he had begun his career bolting steel, and he decided that was his mission—to go to Denver and be a bolter again because, as he put it, "Here I will do things I've never done before as a bolter—that no one has ever done before as a bolter." Another man, a supervisor working on the same crew, was supposed to retire last year. When *he* saw the building, he decided he wanted to be a part of it, so he postponed his retirement. When the extension is finished, I will see it glow from within, with the energy and spirit of those who have poured their labor, and their souls, into it.

The people who dragged the giant stones to Stonehenge imbued them with their big spirits. The place has become something of a degraded tourist site, but if you look past that, you can see that the stones maintain some miraculous conversation with the world. Who were the people who put Stonehenge together? What was it about the particular place, the particular field, that made them bring the stones together and erect them there? And what was it meant to be?

This is what really gets to me: They put the stones in a circle—and they hadn't yet invented the wheel.

The Denver Art Museum houses a perfect sphere carved long ago from a huge stone by people in what is now Costa Rica. Such spheres are found all over the Diquis region of that country, and range from the size of a tennis ball to twelve feet in diameter. The stones from which the spheres are carved are not found in the Diquis region; they had to be quarried elsewhere and rafted in from a distance. No one knows what they are or how they were made or what they represent. They are as much a mystery as Stonehenge, as Mona Lisa's smile.

Trust the Invisible. That's what my father taught me. He had many stories to back him on this, but my favorite is the one of Nachman and the Whistle.

My father was an incorrigible whistler. He could imitate
the song of any bird, and even as a very old man, he could
whistle the Yiddish tunes he learned as a child in Lodz.
(In fact, to guarantee that his beloved songs did not fade
away with him, he invented a form of musical notation
and in his final years meticulously transcribed them and
gave the transcriptions to YIVO, an institute for Jewish re-
search.) A good whistle, my father thought, was like traveling at all times with your own musical instrument—your
own flute or Jew's harp.

Sometimes whistling brought him salvation. It could also
bring him pain.

In 1928, when he was nineteen, Nachman and his best
friend developed a whistle they could use to find each other
in a crowd. One night, the streets were surging with Bundists
on their way to a rally, and the secret police were out in force,
looking for any pretext to make arrests. Nachman's furtive
whistle gave them one. With that whistle, they claimed, he
was sending a secret message to hidden communists; it was a
tool to incite. Nachman was a Bundist and hated the communists, with their totalitarian goals and violent methods.
But that political nuance was beyond the Lodz police, who
tossed my father in jail.

Thirty prisoners—all political activists—were crammed
into a small, windowless cell to await trial. There wasn't
enough space for all to lie down to sleep, so they slept on top
of one another, "like herring in a can," my father said. Even
worse, inmates were not allowed to speak to one another, and

they were monitored by truncheon-swinging guards who made sure that the rules were obeyed.

Leaning against the side of the cell one day, Nachman noticed a tiny hole in the thick wall. Pressing his ear to it, he heard a faint noise from the other side; it sounded like someone breathing in the distance. "Anybody there?" he whispered, when no one was looking. At once came a series of taps: *Yes*.

The two muzzled prisoners developed their own version of Morse code. In an intricate system of taps, they revealed to each other personal details of their lives, and they shared their dreams for the future—a future that would prove much bleaker than they could have foreseen. This was, after all, 1928.

In the middle of my father's cell was one bucket in which all thirty prisoners relieved themselves. The stench was unspeakable, and the only respite came during the twenty minutes the prisoners were let out of the cell each day—long enough for a run around the courtyard to keep the blood circulating. And there was a daily ration of cigarettes, which served to mask, though only very faintly, the unbearable odor.

My father never smoked, so he offered his ration to his new friend, who smoked like a fiend. The challenge was to get the cigarettes through the hole in the thick wall. My father, the whistler with good lungs, quickly perfected the technique of shooting each cigarette through the hole in a single exhalation, like an Amazonian dart-blower.

Because the pretext for which he had been imprisoned—

whistling in public as a political act—was so patently absurd, and because he faced twenty years for it, Nachman's trial became something of a show trial. He was successfully defended by the two most famous Jewish lawyers in Poland at the time, Henryk Erlich and Viktor Alter, who would later flee to Russia, where they would be arrested on spurious charges and made to sign false confessions. It is said that Stalin personally ordered their executions.

My father went on to endure and survive a lengthy series of challenges. Among the very worst, he would recount, came during the early years in postwar Lodz, when he was desperate for work and couldn't imagine how he would support his wife and two small children. One day, too poor to afford a jacket, Nachman stood shivering in a long line of men trying to land a job in a textile factory. A man walked down the line, shouting his name.

"Libeskind! Where is Libeskind?"

My father held his breath. Being singled out like this could mean serious trouble with the UB, the Polish secret police. He steeled himself and stepped forward.

"The *nachalnik* wants to see you," said the man, using Russian slang to refer to the boss.

Stricken with terror, my father followed him into the large office of the *nachalnik*, who rose from his chair to greet Nachman. My father stuck out his hand, but the stranger ignored it. Instead he wrapped my father in an embrace. "Nachman Libeskind! I've waited so long to meet you!" the man said tearfully.

Nachman remained puzzled until the factory boss rapped his knuckles in a rhythmic pattern on his desk. At once my father knew who he was—the man from the other side of the prison wall, from almost twenty years before!

Unlike my father, this man had been a true communist, and as such had been treated well by the party after the war. Now he was the boss of this textile mill, and he had seen Nachman's name on the list of job applicants. And that is how my father came to land the much-coveted job of factory manager. All because of a whistle and a knock, and a faith in the Invisible.

·9

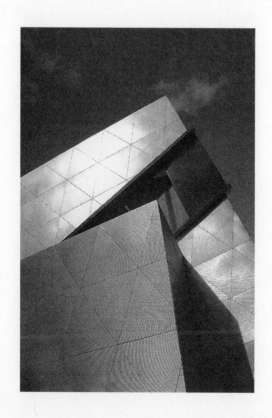

I once invited the marvelous dancer William Forsythe to meet with a class I was teaching. I wanted him to talk to my students about the parallels between choreography and architecture; I wanted them to hear his thoughts about space, which is fundamentally what both are about. Billy is an American-born dancer who went to Europe in the 1970s and, as the artistic director of Ballett Frankfurt from 1984 to mid-2004, set about revolutionizing the hidebound and *über*-traditional world of European ballet. Billy is handsome and funny and original, but he's probably not the first person people think of when they want to teach about architecture. Still, I suspected he had much to say about it, and he did.

I introduced him, he stepped to the front of the room—and he fell down. He stood up. He fell down again. Stood up, fell down. He did this for forty-five mesmerizing minutes, and each fall was absolutely different from the previous one. Forsythe is a consummate artist, and he had the technique to fall in a continually unexpected way. The students were transfixed.

At the end of the class, Billy stood up and said, "And that's what ballet is all about." Which is true, but the students also understood that this was what all art is about: With few tools, and in apparent defiance of gravity, one can repeatedly reinvent the universe.

Painters have their colors, musicians their sounds, writers their words—thousands of them. Although we can design buildings in our heads or on paper, the tools of architects are less easy to assemble. These are my tools: stone, steel, concrete, wood, glass. And the challenge before me is to design expressive buildings—buildings that tell human stories—with these mute substances. Like a dancer, I am acutely conscious of gravity, and I find it remarkable that these materials come from the earth. What is concrete? It's the earth. Glass? The earth. Wood, steel—they come from the earth. Architecture, I realize, is about assembling various components from the earth into visibility.

Each material has its own language and poetry, the cadence of which shifts when it is put alongside other materials. How do this stone and that glass look together? If wood is introduced into the equation, does it change the atmosphere of the place? What does it do to the temperature of a room? What about the light? How does light land, shift, dance along an interior? Stone, glass, wood, light—these are the humble ingredients architects can use for a higher purpose, to express ideas and emotions, to tell stories and chart histories.

Sometimes the stories that materials tell are direct and fairly logical. Most visitors to the Felix Nussbaum Museum, for instance, quickly grasp the nuances of the materials used in the three sections, or what I call "volumes," of the building. They understand why the first volume, devoted to Nussbaum's work from the prewar years, is made from oak, and why it stands close to the old site of the synagogue on Roland-strasse, which was burned in 1938. And it makes sense to them that the second volume, which cuts violently into the first, should be made of blunt concrete. This is the Nussbaum-gang, the cramped passage in which the works Nussbaum painted while in hiding are displayed. The Nussbaum Passage leads to the final volume, this one of metal, which holds newly discovered paintings by the artist.

Materials can of course tell less explicit tales. Take the zinc cladding of the rooftops of Berlin. Zinc is cheap, malleable, easy to produce; it weathers well, can be painted, and is easy to install. That is why, in the nineteenth century, Karl Friedrich Schinkel, the city's preeminent architect, and something of a radical in the Prussian era, suggested that Berlin's rooftops be covered in zinc. And that, amazingly, is what happened.

When I was building the Jewish Museum, I decided to pay homage to these rooftops, and clad the museum in thin sheets of zinc. There are talented craftsmen in Berlin who specialize in the nineteenth-century art of applying the material. Still, the craftsmen and Schinkel notwithstanding, many people said I was making a terrible mistake. It's too flimsy, they warned; it turns bluish. Ah, I told them, but that's what I want: I appreciate that it's a modest material; I appreciate that it slowly oxidizes, and then sort of disappears. I'm not looking for a stainless steel that stays forever shiny. I want the building to blend into the city. I want to see how the windows, with their sharp angles and slashing effects, become even more emphatic as the building softens.

I want my buildings to have an organic relationship to the space in which they live, to relate to the streets and buildings around them—in material, scale, and color. It hurts to look up at the Time Warner building on Columbus Circle; the dark gray glass structure falls so heavily to the street that it feels like a massive shroud, depressing the surrounding area. And I want my buildings to age gracefully and naturally. Facelifts or false fronts are as phony on buildings as they are on people, creating masks that only emphasize how out of synch they are with the core. Do you really need this much space? Do you really need such glitzy materials? When we talk about sustainability, it should be seen as something genuine, not trendy or technically gimmicky. Corporate architects are obsessed with high tech—they love polished glass connected by tension wires. But such tricks are expensive, and we have to ask: Why are we using these materials in this way, and to what effect?

I am not alone in recognizing the achievement of Mies van der Rohe's Lake Shore Drive apartments in Chicago. But to me they are the ultimate irony. When they were built, from 1948 to 1951, they were to be the embodiment, the visual articulation, of the modernist ideology. That was what we were to see in the clearly expressed steel skeletons and the black-painted steel sheets covering the columns and beams. But Mies knew the steel couldn't be fireproofed and thus had to be encased in concrete. And then he covered the concrete with steel—just for show. So much for the idea that form follows function.

Another Chicago skyscraper story: I recently stayed in one of the high-rise hotels there that deploy sophisticated engineering, in a room at a towering height. I opened my curtain in the morning to look out on the Loop below, and what I saw instead were spiders—hundreds of them, dangling from their webs. And I thought, "How wonderful! I'm floating above the city, and nature has made its way up here." The perfect plate glass had been intended as an invisible shield, but nature refused to cooperate, and I was looking down at the city of Chicago through a curtain of spiders. Such poetic justice! The spiders presented a little parable: You can try, but you cannot dominate the earth with architecture.

Many of my buildings are difficult to describe, but that's because they're as much about the experience of being there—

the atmosphere, acoustics, temperature—as they are about the step-back-and-look-at-me aesthetics. A well-designed building has an energy that is transmitted through its space, whether by vibrations that are audible, such as footsteps or voices that travel across a room, or optical, as in the way a staircase or doorway presents itself, or physical, like the feel of the floor beneath your feet.

An American artist named Barbara Weil contacted me about building a space for her in which several different experiences could take place under one rather small roof. She had been living on the island of Mallorca for many years, and now she wanted a villa near her house in which she could paint, sculpt, exhibit her art, and accommodate friends when they came to visit. She wanted more than a regular art studio; she wanted uplifting and energizing spaces for contemplation, work, and the presentation of her art. She imagined that the villa would have a traditional Mallorcan feel, but with a contemporary quality and beauty. And she didn't have a big budget.

The villa that I designed is unorthodox. The interior is a series of concentric but imperfectly shaped rings, which suggest circular islands floating within the exterior wall. The shape is an homage to Ramon Llull, a fascinating and influential thirteenth-century mystic and theologian who lived on the island before he went off to try to convert Moors and was stoned to death in Tunis in 1315. I've been intrigued by Llull for a long time—he was obsessed with memory, and he produced a mechanical contrivance made of concentric wood and metal disks stacked one atop another, which had key words inscribed in them, and which, if used properly, would serve as the supreme mnemonic device. It would take pages to describe how this ingenious if eccentric "logic machine" worked, but it's fair to say that Llull could be credited as the first person to have conceived of a computer.

The form of the device—the concentric rings—provided the inspiration for what Studio Weil would eventually look like, and more than that, feel like. Inside the villa, the working space, studio space, and private spaces appear to revolve around you like moving panoramas; and like Llull's device, which was concerned with memory, the villa's interior seems to bore deeper into itself, tranquil refuge from the outside world.

The house has many other unusual features, not the least of which is that there are no obvious windows to speak of. Though it resists the cliché of landscape merely as beautiful background, it celebrates its site in a contemporary way. I designed recesses in the façade in which the window glass was placed horizontally rather than vertically, to create a self-shading effect and give an airiness to the house. The project is not easy to put into words. But it was a joy to construct, and that to me is what architecture should be—a language of joy and history, that can awaken your own thoughts.

Nobody has captured that awakening as exquisitely as Marcel Proust in *Time Regained,* when the narrator trips against "the uneven paving-stones in front of the coach-house." Until that fateful moment, for almost 3,500 pages, the narrator of *Remembrance of Things Past* has grown increasingly full of despair, and is convinced that he cannot, and should not, write. Then, suddenly, "when, recovering my balance, I put my foot on a stone which was slightly lower than its neighbor, all my discouragement vanished." And in that instant of intense sensory memory, "as if by magic," he recalls the sensation of standing on two uneven stones in the baptistery of St. Mark's in Venice. He realizes that he is experiencing the same particular sensation he experienced years before, when the taste of a madeleine brought back memories of his childhood. This moment, in which Proust realizes he is going to write his book, is for me profoundly architectural. A whole world of sensations, "all of which had been waiting in their places," was waiting for the inherent meaning and structure—or architecture—to be revealed. The shaping of space is important because it engages the body and the mind, emotion and intellect, memory and imagination.

Proust was inspired by common paving stones and his beloved madeleines. I find myself inspired too by ordinary materials, by reinforced concrete, say, or a hunk of steel. Here's what I'm not impressed by: expensive materials like gold leaf, chrome, or marble.

I remember arriving with Nina at the New York headquarters of Skidmore, Owings & Merrill for our first meeting with David Childs about the World Trade Center site. SOM is at 14 Wall Street, an appropriately corporate address for a big corporate firm. As we entered the white marble lobby, I instantly regretted that I didn't have my sunglasses. I was blinded by the white—white marble, white walls, white carpeting, white table, white Breuer chairs. The receptionist was white and dressed in white—or perhaps that's just the way my sensory memory has recorded it. Certainly there was nothing around her. We gave her our names, and she said we would have to wait. I felt as though I were in a morgue.

"Let's get out of here," I whispered to Nina.

"Daniel, be serious," she whispered back.

I was.

In contrast to the razzle-dazzle of high-tech modernism, I think back to Zakopane and the majesty of Poland's primeval forest nearby. Bison roamed the dark, rustling labyrinth formed by hectares of poplars and maples. Dressed in local peasant clothing, my sister and I would explore the bogs and glens, and search for blueberries in the undulating "silver fields," as the poet Adam Mickiewicz called them. Even as a child, I was awed by the forest's magical beauty, and it was there that I began to understand land and space and shelter and the materials of the earth—all the things I would focus on as an architect later in life.

It was in Zakopane that I began to draw, secretly at first. I drew knights, ghosts, and beasts—lions, snakes, bears, mythical monsters. An acquaintance of my father's, Mr. Besterman, used to send Ania and me comic books from the United States, and I spent hours copying the figures from those pages, over and over—Pluto, Mickey Mouse, Snow White and the Seven Dwarfs.

I must tell the story of how Mr. Besterman came to send us the comic books. When my father was released from the gulag on the Volga, he traveled south by train. The trains came infrequently, and when they did, they were packed. And so refugees would line the station platforms for hours, sometimes even days and weeks, waiting for transport to come. One frozen day, from the end of one platform my father heard a wail—the inconsolable wail of a man who knows he's about to die, as my father later told it. He went to investigate, and found the sobbing Besterman, a young Polish Jew. He had fallen asleep, and as he slept, someone had stolen his shoes—which in the Russian winter was tantamount to a death sentence. For my father the answer was simple—he had a pair of used shoes, and he gave them to Besterman.

Mr. Besterman never forgot my father's generosity. He was lucky to leave for the United States before we did, and he thanked my father every year with a package, dispatched from Macy's (which we pronounced with a hard *c*), full of chocolates, toys, and comic books. My parents sold the chocolates to pay for necessities. But they always let us keep the toys and comics.

As my hand grew more assured, I took to lampooning the public figures I found in my parents' newspapers—Khrushchev, Mao, Eisenhower, John Foster Dulles, Mendès France, Ben Gurion. I don't know how I sensed that these caricatures were subversive, but I did, and I sketched in the hidden shade of a big oak tree some distance from our country hut.

Enchanting as the forests of Zakopane were, nothing there prepared me for the natural splendor of the cornfields and orange groves of Kibbutz Gvat, in Israel, where we moved in 1957. The kibbutz—which is still in operation—had risen in the Jezreel Valley, amid the Jewish town of Afula, the Christian town of Nazareth, and the Muslim town of Jenin. My mother's sister Chava, who had moved to Israel in the 1920s, lived at Gvat with her family, the Rogels, many of whom remain stalwart members of the kibbutz. I loved it there, even if the work was sometimes enervating and dull. Corn—I'd never known of it before. Bananas, dates, citrus—fruits I'd never dreamed of, much less heard of. All I recognized were potatoes, which we definitely knew in Lodz. I went swiftly from city kid to serious participant in a real agrarian experiment, thinking about ecology, resource management, sustainability—concerns that would become important to me later, when I was grown and in business for myself. When you've lived on a kibbutz in the desert, green architecture means a lot more than making sure you don't use endangered woods.

We had fled a supposedly communist country, only to find ourselves in a true one. Kibbutz Gvat was communism in practice. Everybody lived in identical spartan concrete bungalows, wore identical clothes, and shared what little they had. When we showed up from Poland with a few bottles of perfume as gifts, the recipients almost sent us packing in outraged disbelief. It wasn't simply that the presents stank of bourgeois values—there weren't enough bottles to go around equally. The children lived in communal dormitories according to age group. It may have been forward-looking, but it smacked of an orphanage, and occasionally my mother would sneak Ania and me out at night to sleep in her room. My father, with his generous soul, would have been content to live on the kibbutz forever, but after life in the gulag and communist Poland, my mother had had it with collective living. She escaped as soon as she could to Tel Aviv, reestablished her corsetry business there, and brought us to the big city. It surprised few people when we left for New York within two years.

Dora could not be stopped. She had an entrepreneurial spirit, and she appreciated quality, whether in handmade undergarments or French perfume or a dig-your-teeth-into-it argument or a side-splitting joke. So would she have been impressed by the white marble at SOM headquarters? Not in a million years. How about by the $1,000 doorknobs that Richard Meier installed in his Perry Street condos? In a world where so many people can't find a decent place to live, Dora would have found them shameful.

It is not the richness of materials that is important, it is the richness of ideas. So yes, part of my resistance to ostentatious opulence is a product of my past. Another part is perhaps a matter of taste.

But glitz is what the client wants, some architects say. Maybe. But I often think that's because the client isn't offered an alternative or asked the right questions.

A potential client comes in. "I want to build a building," he'll tell me.

"Okay," I'll say, "let's discuss what you have in mind."

For some architects, this means: How much will I earn from this job, and what do you want me to do? This isn't what I want to know. I want to know: What is the building for? What is it about? Why is the client interested in making this kind of investment?

What the client invariably tells me is that he wants much more than just a building. He wants more than architecture; he's looking for life. He wants some undefined quality in his building. He doesn't want just an office building, he wants a place where he can feel good working while making money. He doesn't want just a school or a hospital, he wants a place where people can enjoy being educated or feel comforted while being healed.

People always envision great conversations taking place in the building they are commissioning.

I was under consideration to design a giant shopping and wellness center in Brunnen, outside Bern, Switzerland. I met with the client—a group of businessmen—three times. I brought them sketches and models, and by the last visit they were very excited by my design. This is perfect! they said. Where did this concept come from? What is behind the idea?

It was very simple, I told them. It all came from a Marx Brothers film, *The Big Store*. "I love that movie," I said. "I love the Marx Brothers—they're so crazy."

They looked perplexed. So I explained further: "In the movie, the Marx Brothers take over a department store. They hide in the store, and then, after it closes, they invite their friends over and they all start using the beds and couches and tables and chairs and kitchens, until they've appropriated the place for themselves. That's what I think should happen in the store of the future."

I was talking about the atmosphere I would create. And the businessmen got it.

"Yes!" they said. "This is exactly what we think." We agreed that the store of the future isn't going to be only about shopping. The store of the future will be claimed by people who want the place for themselves; they won't just want all the goods there, but will actually want to spend time there, enjoy life there, for hours every day. Like the store in the Marx Brothers movie, this will be a new social space, one that can't be confused with venues for mere consumerism or trendy shopping.

The other architects being considered for the job had talked with these businessmen about merchandising and shopping habits, but the businessmen weren't interested in such discussions. They knew how to sell things. They were interested in something else, I won the commission, and the project is now under construction.

Sometimes inspiration leads you to invent new and unexpected techniques. The massive Royal Ontario Museum sits proudly, if somewhat dully, on the corner of Queen's Park and Bloor Street in Toronto. Over the years it had come to be afflicted with a malady that strikes many museums: it had become a grand old bore. But then the museum board appointed William Thorsell as head, and everything began to change.

Thorsell was not a museum person. A brilliant man, he was the editor in chief of Toronto's *Globe and Mail,* and he is interested in everything: dinosaurs, paintings, textiles, rocks, indigenous people's artifacts. Whatever the Royal Ontario Museum has, he wants it put before the people of Toronto. He even had the idea that the museum should take its most bizarre items—a stuffed bird that no one can identify, because it's extinct; a strangely figurative kitsch Bavarian wood sculpture—and assemble them in an eclectic exhibit recalling the old European *Wunderkammern* and *Kunstkammern,* rooms that displayed items often deemed magical and that were the basis of the modern museum. Thorsell is bringing a sense of fun and wonder back to the museum. And to that end, we are building an extension that will thoroughly transform the historical complex.

Remember the napkins I submitted for the competition for the ROM? After I submitted them, I had an insight that what I had intuitively drawn resembled some of the massive and otherworldly crystals I had seen at one of the museum's exhibits. So in the presentations to the jury, I named my project "The Crystal." The extension tilts toward the sidewalk with striking three-story glass display cases. Not often has a museum displayed on its exterior the treasures found within. In each of these windowlike spaces will be the skeleton of a dinosaur, staring down at the passersby below, like an avant-garde sculpture about to come to life. Imagine what it will look like at night!

To design the outer faces for the Crystal, I took a series of twenty-eight intricately composed drawings I'd made in the 1980s, called *Chamber Works*, and, at Thore Garbers's suggestion, projected them through some large crystals. Crystals are the most perfect forms, and their shapes frequently appear in my buildings. I love the fact that they are luminous, and yet absorb light even as they refract and reflect it. People tend to think of them as complicated, with multiple facets, but a box is a crystal too, albeit simplified. I could talk about crystals for a long time—to me they are miraculous. Ever since I encountered Johannes Kepler's study of the six-cornered snowflake, I have marveled at the infinity of crystals that nature created in every snowflake. Let me leave you with this thought: All architecture is crystalline; architecture, like crystals, consists of solid geometry.

For the Imperial War Museum North in England, I likewise sought to capture the essence of what the museum was about. It was to be built on the Trafford docklands of Manchester, as a branch of the main London institution, exploring the conflicts of the twentieth and twenty-first centuries and their effect on us all. The question was, What should a museum of war look like? How do you explore "Imperial War" without celebrating the failed empire, or in an equally wrong-headed approach, without participating in an antiwar diatribe? I wanted to create a place at once intimate and civic, in which the story of the significance, sacrifice, tragedy, and destiny of conflict could come alive. I wanted the design of the building to have a visceral impact and yet offer a sober setting for visitors to contemplate the permanent reality of war and its bearing on human lives.

It was a challenge, and I had been mulling it over on a visit to London, where I had come to advocate, once more, on behalf of the Victoria and Albert Spiral. To clear my mind, I wandered into a flea market, where I spotted an old globe-shaped ceramic teapot, which I impulsively bought from an equally old lady. I took the pot home to Berlin, hoping it might somehow inspire me and my colleagues. "Let's imagine this is the world," I said to them, and we stared at the poor thing. Then I had a further thought: Ah, the world is shattered by conflict. So I dropped the teapot from the window onto the courtyard on Windscheidstrasse, one story below. We ran downstairs and carefully collected the biggest pieces—the shards, as we called them—and returned to the studio, where we played with them until they fit together in a semblance of a building. Stepping back and studying what we had done, I saw that it worked.

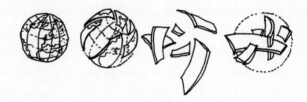

One shard looked like part of the earth's crust. It was horizontal, and it sloped in the same arc as the earth's curvature, so we called it the Earth Shard. The floor of the exhibition galleries would curve gently, just like the surface of the earth. The Earth Shard intersected a vertical Air Shard, whose structure recalled an airplane hangar. At the top would be an observation deck from which visitors could see the city of Manchester and the docklands, still being redeveloped after having been reduced to rubble by Luftwaffe bombing during World War II. A third shard, the Water Shard, would be tilted like a ship at sea. There we would put a restaurant, which would overlook the canal and an old battleship.

Anyone can figure out that with a bigger budget, you can construct a building more easily. But I have rarely had that luxury. Originally, the Manchester museum was budgeted at $50 million. But after we were awarded the commission and were proceeding with plans for the building, the newly elected Labour Party shifted funding from cultural institutions to other projects.

The museum was now in jeopardy, its budget reduced by half. "It's impossible to do this building—scrap what you've done," colleagues and other architects advised me. But I was too deeply committed to walk away, and I decided to accept the budget cut as a further challenge.

On a gray Mancunian day, I met with the museum director, the chairman of the board, and members of the local town council of Trafford. They wanted this building. Despairing over the financial whack leveled at the project, they expected me to announce that I couldn't do the building on such reduced funds. Instead I told them that I would find a way to redesign it and build it, because I believed in their mission. In a four-week effort of extraordinary intensity, I changed the materials, transformed the structure, stripped away the extras, simplified the construction techniques, all without compromising the essential ideas and meaning of the Shards. When I presented the redesign to the town council and the board of the museum, composed of navy admirals and army and air force marshals, I apologized that, with all due deference to conflict, I had to speak softly and without the microphone: my eight-year-old daughter, Rachel, had fallen asleep on my shoulder.

We ended up with a building that satisfied the accountants, pleased the critics, and most important, fascinated visitors, who came in droves and made the museum an instant success. The moral of this story is that reduced budgets can sometimes be the impetus to greater creativity.

I am building buildings today that for the most part could not have been realized in the twentieth century, which is to say just a few years ago. Ten years ago, the structure for the Denver Art Museum extension and the V&A Spiral could have been designed on paper but could not have been built quickly or in a cost-effective manner. Remember, extraordinary cathedrals were built eight hundred years ago, but some took five hundred years to finish. Today, in Denver for example, we have used a computer program that allows the contractor to pick any date during construction and visualize how the various components of the building will come together in the most efficient way, and project how wear and tear will affect the materials used. Such a tool was unthinkable only a decade ago.

It's a given that computers have altered the design process. Is there a drawback to the computer? Of course. In a staggeringly short period I've started having trouble finding young architects who can draw. The computer is their pencil; they are lost without it. Yet the physical act of drawing with one's hand is an important part of the architectural process. An architect needs to know how to draw; unless there is a connection of eye, hand, and mind, the drawing of the building will lose the human soul altogether and become an abstract exercise. I also believe that it's only when they are drawing that architects have those Proustian moments—those instants in which they accidentally trip against the uneven stones of the mind, triggering memories that magically unlock the sorts of visions that underlie all great art. Let there be no mistake: The human hand cannot be replaced by the computer.

Maybe it's the speed of technological advancement in today's world, but I find myself uncomfortably reminded of the Roman Empire. Early Roman engineers already had the technology needed to create the steam engine; they had developed theories of hydraulics and pneumatics, and they used those theories to make funny water fountains, to make the roof on the Emperor Nero's dining room rotate. These engineers never thought about how to put any of their technological know-how to more practical use. They could have developed the steam engine—but they didn't need to, they had slaves to do all the work. So another seventeen hundred years passed before it was invented.

I suspect we're at a similar stage—that computers are being used for games driven by "game theory" when they could, and should, be used for bettering life.

I was recently interviewed for the BBC radio's *Desert Island Discs*, the program in which people reveal which eight recordings they would want with them if they were stranded on an island. My choices included selections from Mozart's *Requiem*, performed by the Academy of Ancient Music conducted by Christopher Hogwood; Beethoven's String Quartet in B-flat Major, Opus 133, performed by the Emerson String Quartet; ancient Greek music performed by Atrium Musicae de Madrid; Giacinto Scelsi's *Pfhat*, performed by the

Orchestra of Radio and Television of Kraków; and Ornette Coleman's *Free Jazz*, performed by the Ornette Coleman Double Quartet.

The BBC interviewer also asked what book and luxury item I would want. Here I chose *Le Carceri*, a series of etchings of prisons as imagined by Piranesi, and as a luxury, pencil and paper. (I regret not having mentioned my bathrobe.)

If I were to compose a list of the most important materials in my life, the single indispensable one, without which I could not build another building, would be Nina.

When I was first working on the Denver Art Museum, I said to her, "This project, I am calling it 'Two Lines Going for a Walk.'" She replied, "What are you talking about? I have no idea what you're saying."

When she said this, I looked at her and thought, What right does she have to ask this? She's not an architect. And then I had a moment of revelation: If my wife has no idea what I'm trying to say, and no idea what she is looking at, then I have to do a better job. We are opposites in every way, and so we complement each other perfectly.

I could design the most magnificent building ever imagined, and could build it with the finest materials ever mined from the earth, but if the right workers weren't building it— if their hearts and spirits weren't in it—the result would be second-rate. When I say "the right workers," this is what I mean:

When I was building the Jewish Museum in Berlin, there were those who warned me that it was a grave mistake to have any exposed concrete, as was planned for the walls of the Void and the Holocaust Tower. "Mr. Libeskind," people said, "this is not Stuttgart or Basel. We are not in southern Germany, which is known for its beautiful concrete work. This is eastern Germany. We have primitive workers, unschooled, untrained. They cannot do the quality work you'll want, and the result will be very, very ugly." But I wasn't worried, in part because I didn't have a low opinion of the foreign workers, who came from Poland, Turkey, Vietnam, and the former Yugoslavia. And I wasn't too concerned also because I didn't actually want pristine quality. If you wish, you can make concrete look like marble. Louis Kahn's buildings look that way, and Tadao Ando's have a similar sheen. But it's expensive to make concrete look like that, and it involves a specialized process and skilled workers. I envisioned, instead, concrete towers that bore traces of human interaction, flaws and all.

But there were very few flaws. Why? Because of people like Andrzej, one of the many Polish construction workers on the site. I started to see him regularly when I visited the museum late at night, to check on progress. We would speak Polish.

"Why are you still here?" I'd ask. And he'd say, "To make sure the concrete is really good."

He diligently checked it every night. When the museum was finished, and I was being considered for the V&A expansion, several people came from England to see my work in the studio and to tour the museum. They marveled at the concrete work. "Wherever did you find the craftsmen?" they asked. "We don't have them in England."

Why was Andrzej's work so good? Somehow the material communicated with him, that's all I know.

One of the most shocking pieces of architecture I've seen is a room at One Liberty Plaza in Manhattan. It is just a plain room in a standard office building, but it overlooks Ground Zero. The room has been set aside for the families of the victims of the World Trade Center attacks, and they have transformed it into a place so powerful that when I walked in, I felt I was entering a dream. They have brought into the room materials that mean something to them—pieces of themselves, pieces of their hearts, pasts, futures. As I stepped inside, I entered the lives of lost souls. I thought: We should keep this at the core of the museum planned for the rebuilt site. It should be left as is, like a secret chamber visitors can enter.

When we look at a city, we make very precise judgments about how it is made, what shape it is in, whether the materials from which it is built will endure or have to be replaced. But the fundamental lesson of New York and of the World Trade Center attacks is a different one: it is that what makes any city strong is not the concrete or steel of its skyscrapers, but the people who live there. Citizens of more than ninety nations died on September 11, 2001, and people from at least as many nations tried to save them. New York derives its strength from the heterogeneity of its population, and from the fact that despite the differences in their traditions, desires, cultures, and incomes, millions of people have come and will continue to come to enjoy the promise of liberty and happiness guaranteed in our Constitution. It is this very promise that the terrorists tried to destroy, but the attack on 9/11 was spectacularly unsuccessful. It did not destroy New York. Nor did it destroy the material promise that continues to quicken 'here and that will continue to draw millions to this great city.

·10

ARCHITECTURAL
RECORD

To The WTC Team:
Now you've done it—cemented a relationship to design the first tower on the former World Trade Center site. We saw the reluctant look in your eyes as you accepted the inevitable and em- braced in the photo-op; we saw the wary resolve and the questions of what lay ahead for you both. We could tell it in your smiles: A forced marriage is never an easy one. You need to know that every architect → → page 19

SHAPING URBAN IDENTITY
The Morphing City
ARE MEGABURBS OUR FUTURE? p. 76
Cincinnati Rising FANFARE
SURROUNDS HADID MUSEUM p. 96

The day will come, I hope, when my three wonderful children have children of their own, and I will be a wise old grandfather who entertains them with the strange stories from my past. And by then, perhaps, I'll have perfected the tale of my forced marriage to the architect David Childs. It will be Homeric (epic in scale, and maybe lasting twenty years or more), Shakespearean (passion! egos! lies!), and will also contain more than a dash of Lewis Carroll, and Alice down the rabbit hole in Wonderland. "Beware the Jabberwock, my son! / The jaws that bite, the claws that catch! / Beware the Jubjub bird, and shun / The frumious Bandersnatch!" And when I finish the story, I'll say to my grandchildren, "What madness, that men behave this way."

The story begins on a spring day in 2003 at Ground Zero, not long after I had won the competition. I visited the site regularly afterward so I could refine my thoughts on the master plan. On one of these visits, I happened to bump into David Childs, who was working on 7 World Trade Center, the replacement for the collapsed Tower Seven. Childs, who is a good few heads taller than I, reached over and gave me a warm hug, as if we were old friends.

"Danny!" A name I hadn't heard since junior high school. "Great to see you," he said affably. "So glad you won! By the way, wouldn't it be a good idea to move the Freedom Tower from where you put it over there"—he pointed to the West Street corner—"to over there"—and he pointed southeast, toward where Church and Dey streets meet.

"Why?" I asked, genuinely curious. To me, such a move would wreck the spiral configuration of the scheme. I wondered what he was seeing that I wasn't.

Childs made a frame with his thumbs and index fingers and squinted through it: "Don't you think it would look better over there?" he repeated. I watched him stare through his impromptu visor.

In light of the their close working relationship, it had been a given that Larry Silverstein would insist that Childs take the lead on the Freedom Tower. To judge from 7 World Trade Center and his Florida condos, Silverstein is not a man who cares much about how things look. The new 7 WTC fills the block, goes straight up, and has a standard façade. The condos are typical Florida. When it comes to buildings, Silverstein likes them big, tall, and ready for business. He had recently gone on a trip to educate himself about world architecture. He visited Japan with Maki Fumihita, and in England he toured Norman Foster's buildings with the architect. When he returned, Silverstein invited Nina and me to his office to meet with Childs and discuss the towers. After describing his trip, he announced that Childs would not be working on all the towers on the World Trade Center site, but that other architects, including Foster, would be involved. "Would I be one of the other architects?" I asked. It was not a rhetorical question. In most cases, architects who win commissions for master plans get the opportunity to design a building on the site—a tower, for example. But Silverstein, who was counting on rebuilding the site with his insurance proceeds, saw it another way. "I don't want you touching my building," he answered. And thus, the battle began.

The fact was, Governor Pataki *did* want me touching the building. He had put himself on the line when he supported our master plan for the site. He personally had named the tower the Freedom Tower, because it was 1,776 feet high, and he believed in the master plan and its symbolism; he felt that the plan and the notions of liberty and freedom on which it was based could help heal New York City. And I think he knew he could trust me; I would be an ardent advocate for the plan and for the public that had supported it.

Because public support was so strong, Silverstein and Childs could not disregard my vision altogether. Instead, they proceeded to circumvent me through less transparent tactics.

In May 2003, Silverstein offered us a lump sum of money and a "consultant" position if we agreed to endorse Childs's design. No, thank you, we said.

Childs's approach was quite different. He proceeded as if contact with us was entirely unnecessary. But after a while, the governor made it clear—to Silverstein, to the Lower Manhattan Development Corporation, and to everyone else involved—that he wanted to see the Freedom Tower built, and soon. To that end, his chief of staff, John Cahill, acting as his representative, called a meeting in mid-July. There, David Childs and I were to come to an agreement that would define and clarify our working relationship.

Nina tracked Ed Hayes down in Florida, where he was visiting his mother. "This is the time you choose to take a vacation?" Nina told him. "Come back. We need you here." Apparently Childs made a similar call to Silverstein's representative, Janno Lieber.

At the end of the workday on July 15, we all showed up at the LMDC offices at One Liberty Plaza. Our two groups were sent to separate conference rooms at opposite ends of the floor. Kevin Rampe, the new president of the LMDC, and Matthew Higgins, its COO, communicated between the conference rooms.

After a few hours of discussion and no resolution, Kevin Rampe suggested that Childs and I meet alone. We went into a smaller room, where we faced each other across a conference table. Childs, who is known for his gentlemanly ways, began softly. "Danny, I gave you the position of the tower.

Larry and I wanted it somewhere else, and we gave you what you wanted." Then his tone changed. "So now I'm going to do the tower I want."

It was hard to know how to respond. "Let's do something great together," I said. "Let's figure this out."

Evidently this was not what he wanted me to say.

"We can make this the next Rockefeller Center," I told him.

"Rockefeller Center is an example of the greatest failure of architecture in New York," he replied provocatively.

"David, you can't be serious."

"It's a horrible project. Doesn't really work at all. It's a great example of planning failure."

Hmmm. Okay. Well. "That's not what New Yorkers think. Then let's come up with some other plan," I said optimistically.

Childs ignored me. I asked him questions, but his answers were neither direct nor responsive. Staring fixedly over my shoulder, seemingly at some spot on the wall, he would answer one question, "Yes, yes, yes," and the next, "No, no, no," and I never quite understood what he was saying.

By now, outside, the lights of the World Financial Center were on. The building had shut down; the air-conditioning had gone off. Hours had passed, and we hadn't gotten anywhere. At a certain point I stumbled down the corridor to the room where Nina, Ed Hayes, and Carla Swickerath were waiting. Ed, uncharacteristically casual in a T-shirt and seersucker jacket, was lying supine on the floor, having come directly from the airport with a raging backache. "I can't believe this," I said. "This isn't working. He won't talk to me. I don't know what to do."

"You gotta make him," Eddie said from the floor. "Although how you collaborate with a guy who wears a yellow bow tie with such an ugly brown serge suit is almost beyond me."

I returned to the other room. "David, look, this thing is bigger than the two of us," I said. "We have to make this work." I told him that this wasn't a stand-alone tower singing solo, but part of a symphony with the four other towers. This was about Ground Zero. It shouldn't be business as usual. "Let me put my cards on the table," I went on. "It's impor-tant for me that the spire is shaped in a way that recalls the Statue of Liberty. And I want the tower to be 1,776 feet high, so the building stands for something substantive, the Declaration of Independence. In the end, this is what mat-ters to me."

"1776! That's a horrible date. To me 1776 is a declaration of war." Childs took off his jacket. "You know what else?" he said, rolling up his white oxford-cloth shirtsleeves. "I think your obsession with the Statue of Liberty is a personal quirk. I think it has nothing to do with architecture."

"How do you see my role here?" I asked. "What should I do?"

At first he refused to answer. Then he made it clear that he was going to, as he put it, "take over the whole site," a sen-timent echoed by others in the SOM machine as they continued to produce drawings for the site plan that were at odds with the agreed-upon master plan.

I went back to the conference room where the others were waiting. Ed, still on the floor, was in a heated argument with one of Silverstein's representatives about the developer's financial responsibilities. Carla and Nina were eating soggy pizza.

"This is insane!" I told them. "Deranged, like out of *The Brothers Karamazov*!" I said.

"Daniel, please," Nina said. "Don't give me this. Tell me what's going on."

I told her what Childs was saying.

"Oh my God." And she began to swear—which she does infrequently but well. She looked fierce when Janno Lieber came in with Kevin Rampe and Matthew Higgins. "We may have to leave," she said.

But neither she nor I had any intention of giving up.

As the newly appointed president of the LMDC, Kevin Rampe had an enormous amount at stake, and he accompanied me down the hall. Leaning into the room from outside, he barked, "David, you must work this out with Daniel." Then he shut the door on us. Thus imprisoned in the conference room, we faced off once again. "I have an intuition of what the building should look like," Childs offered. Okay, this was something. The trouble was, he couldn't really describe his intuition.

"So draw it for me," I said. "You're an architect."

David picked up a pen. He drew a few lines, scribbled over them, then started again. Finally he came up with something that looked like a figure eight. I stared at it, perplexed. "It's like *Bird in Space*," he said. "You know, Brancusi's sculpture."

Ah, so that's what it was. You couldn't tell from the sketch. Later, when I began to visualize the building he was trying to describe, I understood that he was attempting to convey a twisted tower, one that torques as it rises.

It had been hard to grasp what Childs envisioned and how the odd shape he had in mind would ever become a tower. But I could grasp this: His "intuited" tower had nothing to do with the Freedom Tower.

More time passed. Like a Ping-Pong ball, I'd shoot out of the room and down the hall. I'd throw my hands up in despair, and Rampe would send me right back. "Kevin Rampe, don't you try to bully me!" I insisted at one moment. It didn't take a psychic to see how much more fraught things would become; still, Rampe was going to do everything he could to force an agreement that night.

I have to give David Childs credit. He resisted the orders and the pleading of the LMDC. He resisted Eddie Hayes, who is no pushover. No matter who tried, or what their strategy, he held fast. "If this guy doesn't care about what any of us think at this key point," Eddie asked Rampe and Higgins, "do you really think he's going to pay attention later? Do you really think he'll make good on any promise he makes tonight?" Oh, how right Eddie was.

While I was with Childs, Eddie asked for a phone, so he could call Lisa Stoll, the governor's chief of communications and one of his right-hand people, and a very smart woman. It was eleven-thirty p.m., and the governor's office needed to know what was going on. Eddie put the phone on speaker so Kevin Rampe could hear.

"Lisa, we are having a dispute here as to whether or not Libeskind is going to have a significant role in the Freedom Tower," Eddie said. "Does the governor want Libeskind involved or not?"

"There is no debate here, Ed," Stoll replied. "The governor wants Libeskind. The governor wants the Libeskind tower. And the governor wants it to fit into the master plan."

"Thank you very much," Eddie said, and hung up. Rampe nodded and walked down the corridor. He came into the room where David Childs and I were getting exactly nowhere and said: "We've heard from the governor. There's no option. The governor wants Libeskind involved. Are you in or are you out?"

Childs sat silently for just a minute or so, and then said, "Fine." He stood and left the room. "Previous engagement," he informed us on his way out. Janno Lieber stayed on, and by midnight we had reached a preliminary agreement. Our respective roles were represented curiously in percentages, as if the tower's design were a company's stock: SOM would have fifty-one percent of the Freedom Tower design and David Childs would be lead designer, while Studio Daniel Libeskind would have forty-nine percent and be collaborating architect. This cockamamie arrangement increased the velocity with which we continued our plunge down the rabbit hole.

Later, when asked by journalists about our relationship, I described it as a "forced marriage." David Childs was quoted as saying, "We don't want to get swallowed by the Libeskind machine." How absurd. Mindful that he was viewed as Goliath to our David, he had tried to flip the image to win public sympathy. Yet Childs was the captain of one of the world's biggest architectural firms, with offices in New York, Chicago, San Francisco, London, Washington, D.C., Los Angeles, Hong Kong, and Shanghai, while we were around thirty-five people strong with an office overlooking Ground Zero.

"Now you've done it—cemented a relationship to design the first tower on the former World Trade Center site. We saw the reluctant look in your eyes as you accepted the inevitable and embraced in the photo-op; we saw the wary resolve and the questions of what lay ahead for you both. We could tell it in your smiles: A forced marriage is never an easy one."

These were the initial sentences of an urgent "Open Letter to David Childs & Daniel Libeskind," written by Robert Ivy, editor in chief of the influential *Architectural Record*, and published—the first paragraph on the cover itself—in the journal's August 2003 issue.

"Remember what has already happened: the hours of agonizing conceptual design, the hundreds of thousands of dollars spent by the LMDC and other teams of architects," the letter continued. "Despite the gaffes along the way . . . Libeskind's plan emerged relatively unscathed.

"With good reason. Daniel Libeskind captured something beyond mere building in his drawings."

Ivy devoted a portion of his letter specifically to David Childs, urging him not to "cave in . . . [and allow] this site to become a commodified real estate deal." Again addressing Childs, Ivy advised: "If you keep the Libeskind vision intact . . . you may find greatness within your grasp."

He ended with an injunction for the two of us: "Both of you will be tested. Your client, the developer Larry Silverstein, controls the purse strings. The Port Authority, a relentlessly pragmatic institution, owns the land. The Governor of the State of New York holds the political cards. But make no mistake. Ultimately, your client is the public, bound to this place and this process by an ethical trust that you both share."

Throughout history, there have been many truly great architectural collaborations: Bramante, Michelangelo, and Maderna, on St. Peter's in Rome; Philip Johnson and Mies van der Rohe, on the Seagram Building in New York; and yes, Minoru Yamasaki and Emery Roth & Sons, on the Twin Towers. There are all sorts of collaborations, and it's not unusual for even strong egos to work for a common purpose. The architects of St. Peter's collaborated across time, appreciating past contributions and yet extending the boundaries of art.

I have had the good fortune to collaborate with fellow

architects on projects such as the Denver Art Museum, the Imperial War Museum North, the Bar-Ilan University convention center in Israel, San Francisco's Contemporary Jewish Museum, the City University of Hong Kong media center, and the façade for Hyundai headquarters in Seoul. Perhaps the best example is the Milan fairgrounds project, where I am the master planner of the site and at the same time am designing skyscrapers with Arata Isozaki and Zaha Hadid.

I may be among the very few design architects who go out of their way to form joint ventures on almost all their projects; I do this because I thoroughly enjoy the intellectual and artistic interplay between what begins as "them" and "us" and ends simply as "we." So on August 20, 2003, with the encouragement of Robert Ivy and the hope that the collaboration with SOM might prove meaningful, Studio Daniel Libeskind held its first meeting with SOM to plan how the firms would work together. I brought with me Nina, Carla, project architect Yama Karim, and our associate Stefan Blach.

As we were entering the conference room, David Childs studied our small band and said: "We don't need the ladies here today. Today we only need designers."

Excuse me?

"We just need designers here."

"That's fine, I'll leave," said Nina, not inclined to have a fight at our first meeting. "But Carla is an architect. And she's our CEO."

"Well, our CEO is not here. She'll have to go."

I was shell-shocked as my COO and CEO were escorted

away, down to the lobby, where they would sit, working on mobile phones, until I returned more than an hour later. To quote Eddie Hayes, "Those women were treated like dogs." He said other things too, but I won't quote them.

Here were some of the rules of the SOM game: Nobody from Studio Daniel Libeskind was allowed into SOM's offices unless an SOM staffer with an equivalent title was present. In other words, if we had an engineer with us, their engineer would have to be present as well. If our project manager came, their project manager had to attend too. At the beginning, I was not allowed into the offices unless David Childs was present. Yama asked why. The answer came back that I was intimidating and might gain an advantage over Childs and the SOM staff. Later, we managed to get me in occasionally so that I could review the work with my staff. Nobody from SDL was allowed into the SOM offices without prior permission. Eddie Hayes once showed up unannounced, and I thought they would try to have him arrested. The situation recalled the orchestrated arrangements between North and South Korea at the very tense border at Panmunjom. The only thing that made me smile on those difficult visits was the presence of the guards at 14 Wall Street, who always greeted me with words of encouragement.

I had always seen SOM as the epitome of the corporate architecture firm, but these rules extended far beyond the corporate predilection for hierarchy. This was downright nuts. It was weird to inhabit David Childs's universe, where everybody knew his or her prescribed place.

We agreed to hold weekly meetings for an hour every Tuesday morning. The meetings were surreal and often felt like black comedy. I missed the first few because, with Childs traveling, I wasn't allowed to attend. But when he was present, his strategy was to filibuster. For around forty-five minutes he would chatter on about where he'd just been or would lecture me on architecture. During one meeting he started to instruct me on the New York grid. (I guess he thought someone from the Bronx was not from New York.) Perhaps he forgot that we were working in lower Manhattan, where the different patterns of blocks are dictated more by history than by will. His digressions were masterfully effective if transparent strategies to allow little time for, and thereby shut down, meaningful discussion.

After one early meeting, Childs astonished me. "I hear you got fifteen hundred people when you spoke at the National Building Museum in Washington recently," he told me softly. "Largest audience ever, I heard. Bigger even than Frank Gehry. That's impressive, Danny. That's a lot of people." He chuckled, then paused. "You've become very popular." He sounded less warm, more hard-edged. And then his tone changed again. "Danny," he said in an oddly cajoling voice, "after all that I've done, this is *my* building."

After perhaps a month or more of these peculiar non-meeting meetings, we arrived one Tuesday morning to find the walls covered with architectural renderings of a tower at Ground Zero that looked something like a giant corkscrew with a bird on top. No wonder Childs wasn't interested in what we were working on; he was proceeding with plans for the building he had proposed to Larry Silverstein many months before.

This is what Childs had meant when he said he had an "intuition" of what the tower should look like. And this, clearly, is what his staff had been working on all this time. Collaboration? This didn't look like collaboration.

"But David," I reminded him, "we shook hands publicly on a collaboration agreement."

He gave me the patronizing look reserved for the village idiot. "That agreement means nothing to me," he said, with a mirthless smile. "My client is not the LMDC or the people of New York. It's Larry who's calling the shots."

I left the meeting bewildered, confused about how best to proceed and very uneasy about the possibility of disappointing the people who felt strongly as to the kind of building that would memorialize the losses of September 11.

One day I walked to Ground Zero with Childs. Two men recognized me on the corner of Vesey and West.

"So Mr. Libeskind," one of them asked, "where's the tower going to be?"

David jumped in. "Right here!" he proclaimed.

"What's it going to look like?" they asked.

David threw one arm around my shoulder and stuck his other arm into the air. With his outstretched arm and looming height, he had positioned us in a way that deliberately echoed the asymmetrical Freedom Tower I had designed.

But though he now seemed to accept the location I suggested for it, that was the tower he was refusing to work on.

Fortunately, David Childs is not the only architect building on the site. On October 17, Joe Seymour, executive director of the Port Authority, along with Tony Cracciola and others from the agency, met us at the studio of Santiago Calatrava, the architect chosen by the Port Authority to rebuild the World Trade Center PATH station.

I had met Calatrava before. He had visited our office, and I had shown him the master plan. "Ah, I see, it's like music," he'd said. "You have choreographed the space. I know what must be done now."

When I saw the model he presented for the PATH station, I was stunned. "You are an incredible architect!" I told him. His building had giant wings settling on the Wedge of Light, and it was breathtaking—unexpected, just right.

Calatrava embraced the master plan and showed how, for an inventive architect, it serves as an opportunity for creativity rather than as an obstacle. Most important, he understood the symbolic and urban meaning of the Wedge of Light. Every year on September 11, at 10:28 a.m., the time the second tower fell in 2001, the roof of Calatrava's station would open in such a way that the light would filter down into the station, onto the platforms and the tracks below. It was hard not to compare Calatrava's and Childs's approaches to working on this project. Calatrava got it. Childs didn't.

"You are speaking Chinese to them," Yama Karim said as we walked to SOM for one of the weekly meetings. "You keep trying to talk to them about the whole picture. You keep asking what they believe and telling them what you believe. But for them that's not what the process is about. They are each given specialized tasks—one person does the elevators, another works on the lobby. They work in the same big room, but they don't necessarily know how what they are individually doing fits together."

When we arrived at SOM that day, David Childs and his staff greeted us with more than thirty models of antennas. There were antennas in four pieces, antennas in five pieces. . . . The antennas were not entirely a surprise. We had been discussing them for a few weeks. In a real collaboration, choosing an antenna might take a day. In our office, we'd have it resolved in a few hours. But in this alternative universe, who knows? We might pretend to discuss antennas forever. Before we began that discussion, however, Childs launched into a discourse on travel. Something struck my eye as he prattled on about Japan. On the wall was an SOM rendering of the tower.

"How tall is this?" I asked Childs.

"Two thousand feet," he replied. "And this"—he indicated a little mark on the side of the building—"is a flashing light. That's at 1,776 feet."

I was incredulous. My mind went back to the words Childs had uttered—he'd said that 1776 was a declaration of war. Childs well knew that the height of the tower—1,776 feet— was not negotiable. I had told him this. The governor had said so too. As had the mayor. And the people of New York had voiced their support for a tower that stood 1,776 feet tall. The tower would be the tallest in the world, and its stature would never be surpassed.

I didn't know what to do. I wasn't about to give in on the Freedom Tower. So I left. When I arrived at our office, just a few blocks from SOM, the media frenzy had already begun. The "story" was all around town: "Libeskind Walks Out!" declared one tabloid; or as the *New York Post* put it, "Libeskind Storms Out."

"No," I told reporters, "forced marriages can be difficult at first—but we'll iron out our difficulties." In fact, I wasn't so sure.

A flurry of backroom politicking ensued. Ed contacted The Guy. And The Guy contacted Silverstein. The governor's message was clear: The tower had to be 1,776 feet high, and had to look like the Freedom Tower he had selected for the site, and had to be part of the master plan.

Childs, Silverstein, Nina, and I met the next day in a session that was pure Kabuki theater. "You two work out your issues, and do as the governor says!" Silverstein demanded, pounding his desk with his fists. He was trying to impress us with his wisdom and power, but he reminded me of Nikita Khrushchev hammering his shoe on the lectern at the UN. I was under tremendous pressure, and so was the Freedom Tower. Still, I hoped the pressure would lead to something fruitful. A wine press or an oil press, after all, distills the essence while getting rid of the dregs. And architecture, like life, is always under pressure. That is its true nature. To withstand pressure is the essence of integrity, for a human being or a building.

Soon after this meeting, Nina had lunch with Janno Lieber at the Harvard Club, at his invitation. She said that he looked pale and agitated. "This is going to be either very simple," she told him, "or excruciating. But before we leave lunch today, let's agree on the principal design elements that must be included in the Freedom Tower." Janno produced a piece of paper.

"Number one," said Nina, "the building must be 1,776 feet tall. Number two, the roof plane has to continue the ascending spire of the other four towers, making the skyline gesture to the importance of the memorial. Number three, there has to be an ecological component in the sky connecting the roofline to the antenna. And number four, the building has to be asymmetrical, so that it mirrors the Statue of Liberty's torch."

"But David Childs says you can't build an asymmetrical tower," Lieber replied.

"What does he mean, you can't make an asymmetrical tower? I. M. Pei did it fifteen years ago for the Bank of China in Hong Kong. Why does he say these things, Janno?"

Lieber stared into the bread basket. How could he possibly answer this question?

I remember going for a walk with my daughter around this time. We were crossing Central Park West when a policeman waved me over. I turned to Rachel and said, "What could I have possibly done wrong?" As we approached, the policeman took out his ticket book, handed it to me with a pen, and said, "You're the guy doing the 1776 tower, aren't you? Can you sign an autograph for Officer Herrera?" Such unsolicited support helped enormously, and at the end of each week, we'd take a deep breath and resolve to keep going. Though our battle was finally successful, these were most exhausting weeks. Determined as we were to preserve the Freedom Tower, the struggle itself felt like a fight for freedom.

Working with developers can be tricky. It means fulfilling two opposite goals, giving the developer his maximum profits while making sure that the resulting building goes beyond private interests. The worth of the marketplace is enhanced by buildings that add to the cultural and economic success of a place. Industrialists like Carnegie and Rockefeller became immortal because they invested in an architecture with a civic grandeur. They didn't turn their backs on the city but contributed to it.

With the new understanding we thought we had reached with Janno Lieber and Larry Silverstein, we started again.

SOM's torquing tower had little to do with the crucial matters. We set out to devise a solution that would incorporate every aspect of the SOM tower, while remaining true to our own goals. Working with engineers and experts on antennas, elevators, circulation, and servicing, we produced a detailed design after going through hundreds of architectural models. This, I thought, would be a tower that SOM could be proud of, while it fulfilled the solemn promise I had made to New Yorkers.

With great excitement we arrived one Tuesday morning for our usual meeting, and set up our newest models, drawings, perspectives, plans, elevations, and structural analyses. Lieber, Childs, and the rest of the SOM team walked into the conference room. Childs took one look, and pointedly turned his back.

"Janno, I can't go on, I just can't," he said. Then, in furious silence, he stormed out.

Utterly frustrated and disappointed, I too left the room. The following days were tense. The SOM team refused to speak to our staff, and they worked side by side in uncomfortable silence. Meanwhile Childs was still refusing to budge on the height of the building. I needed to find a way to move forward, to present our case to the governor.

I called Yama and asked him to bring back the models, drawings, and sketches we had made of the SOM building, and to try to take photographs of the building within the site model. Some of the SOM staff assisted in bringing the model into the conference room and very generously supplied the photo lights. When Yama and his team returned to the office, we reviewed the material. I had no premonition of the "news" that was about to break.

"WTC's 'Watergate.'" That was the headline in the December 12 *New York Post*. We were shocked. The paper reported that "Larry Silverstein's Freedom Tower design team was so upset over an alleged raid on their offices by staffers of Ground Zero planner Daniel Libeskind that they brought in former Police Commissioner Howard Safir to investigate, sources said yesterday." *An alleged raid!* This was true insanity.

SOM had accused us of stealing our own work, our own drawings, sketches, and models! Outrageous! Another bullying tactic. The *Post* ended its story by clarifying that SOM and Silverstein had called Safir as a "precaution"; they had not "pressed the issue with Libeskind." My staff nonetheless felt insulted, demeaned, defamed.

But we had precious little time before we were to unveil the Freedom Tower to the governor—and the nation. Governor Pataki had picked a date, and there was no delaying it.

Meanwhile, our relationship with SOM devolved from architectural collaboration to political negotiation. I continued to find consolation, and strength, in the people of New York.

Everywhere I spoke—and I was invited to do plenty of public speaking—crowds responded to my ideas about liberty, the Statue, freedom, and a 1,776-foot-tall Freedom Tower.

We had made progress: slowly but surely a design for the tower that was a hybrid of SOM and SDL emerged. Childs agreed to the asymmetry for the tower and to our plan for a series of buildings whose roofs sloped toward the memorial site in an ascending spiral. I had to make one major concession, which still troubles me. Because the tower torques, and therefore each floor becomes progressively smaller as the tower rises, delivering Silverstein's required 2.6 million square feet meant that the bottom twenty floors had to be much larger than in a standard skyscraper. I wouldn't have cared, except that the SOM building removed the space I had designed as the Park of Heroes, dedicated to the heroic police officers, firemen, and other emergency workers who so bravely gave up their lives on September 11, 2001. This was a fight I lost.

There was one key battle left, which I addressed in a final meeting, which Ed Hayes helped to arrange. It took place in the governor's office. John Cahill, Lisa Stoll, and the LMDC's Kevin Rampe and Matthew Higgins were there. I sat with Nina, Carla, Yama, and the ever-supportive Eddie Hayes.

"We're almost there," I told the group. "The tower is in the right location. The rooftop slopes at the right height—and in the right direction, toward the memorial. Childs has agreed to an asymmetrical tower. Instead of the gardens we proposed, he has offered windmills, which we think are terrific. Just one problem remains: Childs won't budge on the tower height. I want him to bring it down to 1,776 feet, as we originally agreed. And I want that spire to be shaped to evoke the Statue of Liberty." I explained that at 2,000 feet, with windmills on top, the tower would be monstrously out of proportion with the rest of lower Manhattan, and would cast a shadow over the entire neighborhood.

As we discovered later, after we had left the meeting, Cahill and Stoll called Governor Pataki and told him what had transpired. The governor responded by phoning Childs directly. He told him to bring the building down in height and to make sure the spire would be evocative in the way we had all agreed on.

A few days later, once he had submitted to the governor's directive, David Childs told me, "You spoiled my tower."

"No, David," I said, "I improved it. I made it into something significant."

On December 19, 2003, at Federal Hall, where the first U.S. Congress met and wrote the Bill of Rights, and where George Washington was inaugurated as president, Governor George Pataki, Mayor Michael Bloomberg, Larry Silverstein, David Childs, and I joined hands and pulled a cord to reveal a nine-foot-tall acrylic model of the Freedom Tower, which will soar 1,776 feet into the New York sky.

· 11

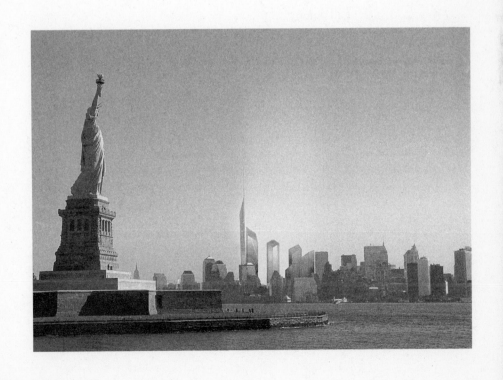

faith

You can be a melancholic musician and compose in a minor key. You can be a writer with a tragic view, a filmmaker obsessed with despair. But you cannot be an architect and a pessimist. By its very nature, architecture is an optimistic profession; you have to believe, every step of the way, that from two-dimensional sketches, real and inhabitable three-dimensional buildings will emerge. Before millions of dollars are committed, and years of many people's lives, you have to know, really know, that the building that results from all the money and effort will be worth the investment, will be a source of pride, and will far outlive you. In the end, architecture is built on faith.

On July 4, 2004, some seven months after we presented our plan for the Freedom Tower, we attended the official groundbreaking ceremony at Ground Zero. When the twenty-ton granite cornerstone was unveiled, we read the following inscription: "To honor and remember those who lost their lives on September 11, 2001 and as a tribute to the ENDURING SPIRIT OF FREEDOM." Later the stone was lowered into its final resting place, in the northwest corner of the site, where the Freedom Tower will rise.

People ask, "During your struggles over the design and master plan, were you ever tempted to throw in the towel, to walk away from the whole thing?" I say, "No—at least, never for more than a moment." And this is why: I never lost faith that the spirit of New York would override individual concerns and that what would finally emerge from the turbulence would be wondrous and healing.

People say too, "Well, you must hate it that you had to compromise so much." I must make this clear: There have been far fewer compromises than people imagine, and besides, compromise is an integral part of the architectural process. I am particularly gladdened that I helped ensure that the site will remain a meaningful place, one that addresses the past but speaks to the future; that it will never be a Potsdamer Platz, where history is ignored and submerged. Together, the memorial, towers, public spaces, and the PATH station form a coherent landscape infused with a sense of place and history, yet one that is also forward-looking and full of life. The site will be a testament to what happened, to who we are, and to what we believe.

In New York, everybody knows everything. Every setback and every rift has been reported. People know we've had serious, sometimes ugly, disagreements with Larry Silverstein. They know there's little love lost between Skidmore, Owings & Merrill and Studio Daniel Libeskind. But what the public cares most about is how Ground Zero will be rebuilt.

The entire site is conceived as a model of sustainability for the twenty-first century. The aim here is not to replicate the

exploitation of the environment that we saw in the twentieth century. The tough design guidelines that are part of the
master plan will dictate our ecological approach to every
building and every public space, to ensure that renewable energy sources, "intelligent" buildings, and sustainability are
not mere phrases but exemplars of urban development.

It was central to the integrity of the master plan to provide the largest possible space on the site, to guarantee that
the public could descend to bedrock, and to keep the slurry
wall visible. After months of assiduous work with the Port
Authority, we managed to carve out and preserve 4.6 acres for
Michael Arad and Peter Walker's pastoral memorial, which
was chosen by an independent jury. When this elegant design
was selected, there were many, including the noted critic Paul
Goldberger, who felt I had compromised too much by ac-
cepting this plan. They were wrong in presuming that the design had subverted my original intentions. The designers
interpreted my vision in their own way—that's what the master plan is all about! The footprints of the two towers are
maintained, and serve as entry points to thirty-five feet below
ground, and one can touch the slurry wall at bedrock.

The Wedge of Light survived the initial rough-and-tumble
of the process, and I am still fighting to keep the plan intact.
When I first suggested it, there was resistance from the developer: Why use so much space for something that doesn't really
serve a purpose—especially when there's already going to be
a memorial? Why do we need more public space? But the pleasure we take in space—both private and public—is not theo-

retical; it is fundamental, to how our cities are organized and built and, ultimately, to how we live our lives, in our communities, in the future. To that end, the Wedge of Light will serve an important purpose: it will be the largest open space in lower Manhattan, which is a streetscape of many narrow and dark roads. Downtown cries out for light, and this grand space, this piazza—which will include Santiago Calatrava's light-filled PATH station—will be rare and special, a gateway, a place for celebration, art exhibits, markets, public gatherings.

One victory in the long battle over the master plan meant more to me than any other: our success in preserving aspects in my design that evoke the Statue of Liberty, and the symbolism the statue embodies. It was a hard-won battle. There were those who never felt the visceral connection to the idea that I did, others who found the connection corny. It set their sophisticated teeth on edge. But to me the Statue of Liberty is not a trinket on a keychain or a piece of rhetoric; it is the personification of liberty, the living flame. I have always had faith that most New Yorkers feel as I do, and embrace, as I do, Lady Liberty's essential message, that of the Declaration of Independence: "We hold these truths to be self-evident, that all men are created equal, that they are endowed by their Creator with certain unalienable Rights, that among these are Life, Liberty and the Pursuit of Happiness." This is not about political orientation but about all Americans.

A Dora story: In 1960, my mother was making thirty-five dollars a week dyeing fur in an unbearably hot, unventilated sweatshop that profited by exploiting poor but skilled immigrant workers, mainly women, who couldn't speak English and were deemed too old to learn. There was no protective gear for those who handled chemicals, and the bathrooms were foul and lacking in soap and towels; workers who wanted to wash up had to bring their own. The conditions were intolerable, but like others, my mother needed the job. She organized a rebellion against both the bosses *and* the union, threatening a strike. The workers won: the sweatshop owners improved the washroom facilities.

One day, Dora found herself in the elevator with the sweatshop manager. "Why aren't you saying hello to your boss, Mrs. Libeskind?" the manager asked testily.

My mother turned to him and said, "Because he never says hello to me and he treats his workers badly."

Just as the commandant in the gulag could have shot her, the manager could have fired her. Instead he shrank away.

I fought for the symbolism of the Freedom Tower on behalf of my parents, and of those whose voices may be quieter than Dora's but whose hearts are just as strong. Everywhere I go, I meet people like them. "How are you doing?" they ask. "Don't give up. We are counting on you."

Cities are made by human dreams. Sometimes we forget.

For the past year or so, while we have been renovating an apartment downtown, Nina, Rachel, and I have lived in a residential hotel in Manhattan. The head concierge is a man named Miguel Abreu, who is from Colombia. He gets his information from the *New York Post*, which has never liked me or my work. But from the moment we moved in, Miguel let me know that he was rooting for me. Despite what he read in the paper, he called out to me every morning as I passed his counter, "Mr. Libeskind! Keep smiling."

And then Garner Cortez would chime in. He's the Filipino doorman. "I hope things are going well," he would say. "My wife follows all the reports."

Hundreds of people have wished me luck or told me about someone they knew of who died at the site, someone's father or brother or wife or friend. And despite all the stereotypes about New Yorkers, no one has ever said anything nasty to me.

Under most circumstances, New Yorkers are practical people; this is the city of the quick buck and of getting on with things. But September 11 was different from anything New Yorkers—or anyone else in the country—had ever experienced, and the events of that day extend far beyond the horror of the almost three thousand lives lost. The image of the two towers collapsing shook our collective unconscious. We take it for granted that buildings this big, this heavy-footed and deeply grounded, will stand no matter what. After September 11, it seemed that all of our foundations, philosophical as well as physical, were under attack and might also collapse.

In some circles it is fashionable to interpret the attacks as the inevitable result of U.S. imperialism, or the nation's oil policy, or its global arrogance. I don't buy that. The strike on the World Trade Center was an attack on democracy—on global democracy and global freedom. New York was a target because it is the center of the free world.

And New Yorkers responded by reasserting the strength of

the philosophy under attack. The public insisted on having a role in the rebuilding of their city. First, some 5,000 people showed up to boo the initial set of proposals for Ground Zero, which they loathed. Then they lobbied hard, and successfully, and another competition was set up. More than 80,000 lined up at the Winter Garden to view the finalists' entries. When the competition for the memorial was held, 5,200 people entered designs. Few were professionals.

In an article in the *The New York Times Magazine* in the late summer of 2003, James Traub drew a parallel between fourteenth-century Florence and twenty-first-century New York. "In 1366," he wrote, "the wardens of the Opera del Duomo submitted to the citizens of Florence a referendum on the construction of the dome of the Cathedral of Santa Maria del Fiore. The wardens had chosen a design that would raise the widest and tallest dome ever constructed without recourse to the buttresses that typically supported great church buildings—an act of boldness they decided required the stamp of public approval. The referendum passed, thus germinating a process that would flower half a century later with Filippo Brunelleschi's extraordinary design for a giant freestanding dome.

"The debate that has unfolded over the rebuilding of the World Trade Center for the last year," Traub continued, "has brought New Yorkers as close as they have ever come to the ancient Florentine conviction that the most profound questions of urban design demand a public voice."

Traub went on to wonder whether this was just a passing

moment of engagement or whether, by so actively participating in the process, New Yorkers had found a new collective voice on these matters. In the future, will New Yorkers
retreat from debate about public space, or will they maintain
a more active role in decisions that developers make about
what kinds of buildings go where? Traub wasn't sure, but he
sensed that something fundamental had changed. "New Yorkers," he wrote, "will never be Florentines—we have more
transitory things than buildings on our minds—but we will remember the World Trade Center attack as a time when the
city began to matter to us in a new way."

Traub is absolutely right.

For the most part, architects aren't democratically minded
people. They admire the cities built by kings and generals. I
suspect there are quite a few who envy Baron Haussmann,
who, despite his very Prussian name and origins, during the
nineteenth century became Napoleon III's prefect of the
Seine, which is to say, the mayor of Paris. Haussmann hated
little winding streets (too easy for revolutionaries to hide in,
he said) and favored broad boulevards and parks (easier to
shoot revolutionaries in, if necessary), so he leveled vast quarters of the city, and drove out the residents, in order to rebuild
as he saw fit. We find these boulevards very beautiful today;
we may have forgotten how they came about.

The fact is, architects usually want the public as far from
the process as possible. Architects and others will tell you
that public participation leads to watered-down schemes, and
mediocre, muddled visions. This hasn't been my experience.

Indeed, I've found that the more transparent the process, the more innovative the result. The only times I've had trouble with building projects were those occasions when I had to deal with the restricting control of one small cabal or one person, such as Herr Stimmann in Berlin.

It is often said that nothing creative is ever produced by committee. But architecture is not a solitary, private art. The Greek root of the word *idiot* refers to, among other things, a private person. The world is not "a tale told by an idiot, full of sound and fury, signifying nothing," but an unfolding mystery. Architecture lives in the world, and it's for the people. Collaboration is about listening to others, learning from them, letting them learn from you. No one can build a huge project alone.

Lewis Sharp, the director of the Denver Art Museum, and William Thorsell, the director of Toronto's Royal Ontario Museum, brilliantly handled the transformations of their respective institutions. Though many museums and other public institutions are built by the edict of powerful patrons and moneyed elites, Sharp and Thorsell understood that an involved public is a precondition for any museum that is truly grounded in the city it serves. They shared the sentiment that architects should be brought before the public, speak before the public, and allow the public to respond. If people wanted to cheer, terrific; if they wanted to boo, so be it; but the public should be involved in the decision. In both cities, great crowds came to see the architects' presentations.

Each man posed his own questions. Lewis Sharp asked:

"What is a museum of the twenty-first century? Does Libeskind's building work for us? Does it work for Denver?" William Thorsell wondered: "Did you really like this scheme? Is it too much for Toronto? Is our city ready for this?" Both men showed faith in the public's ability to make the right decision.

Life is about taking risks. Not long ago, after a lecture I gave, the CEO of the investment banking firm Goldman Sachs approached me. "Goldman Sachs is successful because the company took gigantic risks, which could, at any moment, have ruined us," he said. Later he told a group of people one of the company's guiding principles: Complacency leads to extinction. It's an interesting thought, and I agree with it.

I've always been fascinated by the American Revolution and by the fact that, despite impossible odds, free men rose to defeat tyranny. What temerity to rise against an empire, and one that was held to be unbeatable in world history! This country was founded as a nation of risk takers, and democracy itself is one of the greatest risks; it is an ongoing participatory experiment in which much depends on individuals. Ancient Athenian democracy can be said to have lasted only forty years or so. Ours is among the longest-running democracies in history.

One of the things I admire most about this country is its readiness to experiment and to change. Americans are alive to, and enthusiastic about, the unexpected, and they place a premium on individuality. They see the world as a work in progress. That's the beauty of American pragmatism and American ingenuity.

Architecture needs more adventurers, more risk takers and rule breakers.

Most people imagine risk takers as larger than life, swaggering types. But the greatest risk taker I have known was also the most mild-mannered person I have met: my father. Nachman was an idealist, a utopian in the truest, most lovely, sense. He is the only person I know who seriously studied Esperanto, the universal language introduced in the nineteenth century by Dr. L. L. Zamenhof, a Jew from Poland, who believed that humanity could be united if only we all spoke the same language.

When he was in the gulag, my father was singled out one frigid morning as he stood at roll call. "Nachman Libeskind will step out of line." My father swallowed hard and stepped into his fate.

"Did you write this in your own handwriting?" The commanding officer glared, holding up a prison form my father had filled out when he'd entered the camp.

My father said yes.

"Follow me," the commanding officer said, and led Nachman to the officers' quarters, where my father was told that he had been selected to be the brigade leader for half of the camp. He had authority over four hundred prisoners; another Polish Jew was responsible for the other four hundred. My father had been chosen because of his exceptional handwriting. He had once taught himself calligraphy, and his handwriting looked as if it were printed by machine. When it came time to choose a prisoner as a brigade leader, the commanding officer figured that handwriting was as good a basis as any for selection.

Though it gave him power, the "promotion" was dangerous. Serving as the intercessor between four hundred starving prisoners and their vicious Soviet guards was not a congenial task. Nachman understood that his survival depended on his ability to maneuver between the prisoners and their captors with as much precision as he used in dotting his *i*'s. But he also protected his fellow prisoners. When they begged Nachman to let them off work, he could never find it in his heart to deny them. He filed false reports and told them to stay in bed. He risked his position, possibly his life, to let them rest, because, as he explained, he was one of them, and would have expected another to do the same for him had their roles been reversed.

One of the men my father regularly protected at the camp had been a professional thief in Poland. (He even identified himself as "thief" when camp officers asked his occupation.) The man put his talents to use in the camp; my father described him as a sort of gulag Harry Houdini, a starving confinement artist. He was constantly caught committing petty offenses and thrown into solitary confinement, yet he was able to slip out at night undetected. The man was capable of extraordinary acts of pilfering; he stole precious bread, sugar, and salt from the guards' canteen. But he was also as big as a bear—he could hardly survive on the meager rations doled out, so when the guards weren't looking, my father would give him extra bowls of soup.

The camp was liquidated after the German invasion of Russia. Because of his many kindnesses, my father received presents from the other prisoners when they left. One gave him the most precious of gifts—an extra pair of shoes, the very pair that he would later give to Mr. Besterman.

When we were living in Israel, we went on a pilgrimage to Jerusalem. When we returned to our apartment in Tel Aviv, we found it empty. Everything had been stolen. We were destitute. For a week. Then the doorbell rang, and there stood a giant man holding our stolen radio. Nachman threw his arms around the man. It was the thief from the camp!

After being released from the prison camp on the Volga, the thief had made his way down to the Holy Land, where he'd fought in the war for independence. After the war, he resumed his old career, and even became ringleader for a band of burglars in Tel Aviv, one of whom offered him a cache of stolen goods to fence—our goods. When he learned the name of the household from which the property had been stolen, the former gulag thief brought everything back to us, and joined my father for tea and a round of reminiscing. Despite his honorable action, my mother never let him into our house again. "The Law is greater even than our gratefulness," she said.

"Deep down everybody is essentially good," my mother used to say in Yiddish. I'm not sure she entirely believed it, but that's faith.

In her last years, when the lymphosarcoma was unstoppable and she knew the end was near, Dora secretly wrote the story of her life. The day before she left for the hospital for the final time, my father smelled paper burning. He ran into the kitchen to find my mother crying and fanning the flames of the charred manuscript—hundreds of pages—in a metal garbage bin by the window. He managed to salvage a few pages, which were reprinted as a memorial book after her funeral. Why did she burn it? Were the memories too painful for her in the end? Or did they contain secrets that would have hurt others? My father reveled in telling the story of his life, but Dora kept much of her past hidden and seemed interested only in the present. Perhaps, in writing down her life story, she was exorcising demons from the wreck of her past, and by destroying what she had written she destroyed them. I still wish, with a mixture of curiosity and dread, to know what she burned. I am more like my father in believing that we look forward only if we understand our own stories and our past; that we know who we are only if we know who has come before us.

There's a key moment when you're taking off in an airplane, a "Fasten your seat belt" moment, when you look out the window and see nothing but gray. You're in the dividing line between the lower light of the earth and the upper light above. It's hard to tell if you are going toward or away from the light. That's the most frightening time. In July 2004, as I was writing this book, I decided to brave the grayness of Poland and return for the first time in forty-seven years.

What made me decide to go back? To tell you the truth,

I'm not sure. But I do remember staring down at a letter from
the Zachęta, a museum in Warsaw, which invited me to hold
an exhibition there, and thinking that *zachęta* means "encouragement" in Polish. Maybe it was the sight of that word
in my mother tongue that prompted my decision to return.
Almost without planning it, I landed one evening in Warsaw
with Nina and our older son, Lev, and the very next morning we were in a car on our way to Lodz.

Lodz is still the second-largest city in Poland, but there is
no main highway from Warsaw. To get there, you have to
drive down a series of country roads, dotted by shrines, some
to Jesus, others to the victims of car accidents.

What had happened to the vast city of my childhood?
The proportions were all wrong. I felt as if I were descending
into shoes and streets that no longer fit my body. All the high
buildings I recalled had shrunk. The main boulevards that
had overwhelmed me as a child, full of traffic and jostling
strangers, now appeared quiet and empty.

We pulled up to the Grand Hotel. When I was ten, I'd
been taken inside to see what was then considered the best address in town. I had performed on my accordion here. Now the
building was dilapidated. Every sight, every smell awakened
ancient memories; every doorway, façade, and corner had the
feel of a dusty drawer that hadn't been opened for decades.

We were met by Danuta Grzesikowska, a childhood friend
of my sister's, whom she and my father had visited in the
1990s. Together, we walked to my parents' workplaces and to
the schools Ania and I had attended. What a tight little cir-

cle this turned out to be. As a child I felt as if the city were infinite. Now it seemed everything lay on the same five streets,
perpetually leading back on themselves as in a Möbius strip.

There was the apothecary's with the same grandfather
clock. There was our courtyard, with the same pole that was
used for beating carpets, in the same spot as when I'd left in
1957. Followed by prying eyes, I walked through the courtyard to the last door on the left, and as I looked up at the
second-story windows, our windows, a concrete-colored head
popped out one flight above.

"Do you know if the tenants of the apartment beneath
you are home now?" Danuta asked.

"They're not," the lady crowed. "Won't be back till
tonight. Besides, they're not very nice and won't invite you
in!" She stared at Nina, Lev, and me in our New York attire.

"Do you remember the Libeskind family?" I asked.

After a silent moment, she nodded. "I've lived here sixty-
five years," she said, studying us more. "I am the only one remaining from that time. Nice family, especially the husband.
Little girl, even younger boy . . . he used to play the accordion,
I think. I used to sit at this very window and listen to him."

"That was me," I said.

She who had never left the courtyard and I who had not
returned, until now, eyed each other across the same space,
through the same window, as we had in some forgotten instant nearly fifty years ago.

In the past year I have been to Tunis, and Seoul, and Hong
Kong, and none of them has felt so strange to me as Lodz. So

familiar and yet so strange. Keith Richards, describing the Mississippi Delta blues that inspired the early Rolling Stones, said the sounds were as eerie as Bach. Uncanny and magnificent, yet full of sadness. That's how Lodz felt to me. The city appeared to be made of cardboard, a decaying set for a movie that wrapped long ago.

Architecture is the eternal witness testifying mutely that the past we imagine is not illusory. I really did walk this street long ago, really did knock on that door. But as my son Noam, the cosmologist, will tell you, all matter is hurtling out from a hypothetical center through space at the speed of light, so that we can never really, objectively, be in the same place twice. And space is nothing but an entanglement of strings, a vast Cloud of Unknowing, swirling with visible matter and dark matter and antimatter, where light disappears inside black holes and where impossible Lewis Carroll–type things happen to the laws of physics. Yet it is not to science but to architecture to which we refer when we speak of space or time in relation to our own experience and memory. Architecture expresses, stabilizes, and orients in an otherwise chaotic world.

We walked through the former Jewish ghetto, which had been leveled and filled with Soviet-style housing projects, and passed the palace of the entrepreneur and Industrial Revolutionary Izrael Poznanski, who built his home beside his textile factory, so, like a villain out of Dickens, he could sit at his window in the morning and watch the proles report for work as he sipped his *kawa*. And then we were at the vast necropolis of Lodz, that largest Jewish cemetery in Europe.

It was already getting dark when we entered the poorest area of the cemetery. Danuta led us to the grave of my grandfather Chaim Haskell, which my father and sister had had restored in the 1990s. I was surprised to see that the inscription was in Polish not Yiddish. I assume Nachman had it written that way knowing that there were no Jews left—perhaps he wrote it out for the Polish workers in the cemetery who would likely be the only people to see it.

Now all we had to do was find my grandmother's grave, which was some distance from my grandfather's. After walking down an overgrown and mossy path for about a hundred yards, Danuta pointed past the first row of graves to a second row hardly visible beneath the green. The words of a German poem suddenly came to me—*Green is the house of oblivion*.

The Polish workman who had accompanied us thus far like a silent shadow now, at Danuta's instruction, whipped out his shears and hacked his way through the wall of vegetation, until he reached the tomb. We paid him and he disappeared into the oncoming night.

I bent over the faded inscription. RACHEL LIBESKIND—the name of my daughter. The name is inscribed in Lodz as well as in the future.

In Warsaw, the most revelatory moment for me was at the Zachęta, where I gave a lecture to a packed crowd. The audience erupted in applause as I entered, and more so when I began speaking in Polish. I introduced myself briefly, said how good it felt to be back after so long, and told them that I was rediscovering Polish culture—which is, after all, my culture too. And then I said, "Because my Polish is very rusty, I'll switch to English now," only I forgot to switch. I automatically started speaking Polish again. It was as if that was what my brain wanted to speak. The crowd was delighted and clapped again.

In their questions I could sense an excitement. To them, I wasn't an American Jew or an Israeli. I was a Polish Jew, speaking to young Poles about universal matters—history, memory, architecture. And as I looked out at their youthful faces, I sensed emotionally what I already knew intellectually: This is a new generation of Poles, one that is aware of the evils of the past. They wanted to consider me one of them, and for the first time in my life, I saw that they were part of me.

It is as Dora used to tell me: People are pretty much the same all over the world. When we look back in time, and then at ourselves, we don't see a huge change in human development. Slightly for the better, perhaps. A little bit. You have to believe.

Many years ago, Nina and I made an architectural pilgrimage to Italy to see the Sanctuary of the Holy House in Loreto, a grand project built by Antonio and Giuliano da Sangallo and Bramante, among others. As I entered the church and looked at the extraordinary shrine, I saw in front of me two almost baroque curves cut into the floor. Even with all my knowledge of architecture, I could not at first fathom those strange depressions in the stone. It was with a profound shock that I realized these tracks were created by human knees of worshippers over the years. The power of faith to transform even stone and recompose an architectural edifice was a lesson I have never forgotten.

In Hebrews 11:1, it is written: "Now faith is the substance of things hoped for, the evidence of things not seen." For an architect, these words are profound. We put our faith in things unseen each and every day. As I write this, there are designs of mine that may never be built. The Victoria and Albert Museum, for example, is having difficulty lining up funds for the Spiral. But I never give up hope; I always believe my buildings will be built, and given time, they almost always are. I am enough of a realist to know that they may not stand forever, although I build them to do so. What is more important to me is that each of them captures and expresses the thoughts and emotions that people feel. If designed well and right, these seemingly hard and inert structures have the power to illuminate, and even to heal.

You have to believe.

acknowledgments

My creative rapport with Sarah Crichton while writing this book has been a source of great joy. Sarah's intelligence, insight, and sense of humor have been important to me during the past months, and I thank her for those gifts.

It is seldom that a father, in telling his own story, has the pleasure of depending on a son who is both a writer himself and a scholar. My son Lev was involved from the beginning, helping mold my first ideas about how to tell this story, and helping shape a tale that others might want to read. His passion and support throughout have made this book a reality.

Noam, my younger son, who spends his days in England studying black holes, has been a steady presence while I worked on the book. His scientific curiosity and capacity for wonderment have been an example to me.

My beloved daughter, Rachel, whose stoicism in tolerating two parents whose time is so often not their own, continues to inspire me. With a maturity beyond her years, she has made the transition from Berlin to New York at a difficult time and with a grace that astonishes everyone who meets her.

This book would not exist if my literary agent, Scott Mendel, had not approached me and urged me to share my thoughts about my life and architecture. He has guided me through the labyrinthine process of publishing a book with a care and a devotion that reflect the kind of warm, humane, and widely read human being he is.

As in every other project I have undertaken since 1969, Nina's constant support and superhuman tenacity have inspired me and fueled my determination to tell a story that is as much hers as it is mine.

Working with talented and experienced people has been especially gratifying. So many have given of their professional skills and personal enthusiasm that it is hard to know whom to thank first: Susan Lehman, my editor, who offered this book a home and shared my vision for it; my extraordinarily dedicated publisher, Cindy Spiegel, who has made the book a personal commitment and not merely a professional exercise; Julie Grau, her co-publisher; Cindy's assistant, Susan Ambler; Catharine Lynch, Meredith Phebus, Diane Lomonaco, and Anna Jardine; and Susan Petersen Kennedy, the president of Penguin Group (USA) Inc., who welcomed me under her great big tent. Stephanie Huntwork and Claire Vaccaro are responsible for the beauty of the volume you now hold in your hands.

I thank others at Penguin who have worked and will continue to work on behalf of the book out in the world, including Marilyn Ducksworth, Mih-Ho Cha, Dan Harvey, Steve Oppenheim, Dick Heffernan, Mike Brennan, Katya Shannon, Paul Deykerhoff, Fred Huber, Leigh Butler, Hal Fessenden, and Bonnie Soodek.

Thanks to those at Studio DL involved in the project: David Luther, Benjamin Kent, and Thierry Debaille.

I acknowledge also individuals at publishing houses overseas who made the very early decision, even before I had finished writing, to publish the book in their countries. These publishers and editors took a leap of faith: Lynn Chen, Max Lin, Helge Malchow, Marcella Meciani, Valerie Miles, Alena Mezerová, Etsuko Ohyama, Carla Tanzi, Oscar van Gelderen, and Gordon Wise.